# 20th Century Computers
## and How They Worked

# The Official Starfleet History of Computers

Jennifer Flynn

*Computer Illustrations by Hans and Cassady, Inc.*

*A Division of Prentice Hall Computer Publishing*

*11711 North College Avenue, Carmel, Indiana 46032 USA*

International Standard Book Number:1-56761-257-1
Library of Congress Catalog Card Number: 93-71442

95 94 93    9 8 7 6 5 4 3 2

Interpretation of the printing code: the rightmost number of the first series of numbers is the year of the book's printing; the rightmost number of the second series of numbers is the number of the book's printing. For example, a printing code of 93-1 shows that the first printing of the book occurred in 1993.

Screen reproductions in this book were created by means of the program Collage Plus from Inner Media, Inc., Hollis, NH.

*Printed in the United States of America by*
*Shepard Poorman Communications Corp.*
*7301 N. Woodland Drive, Indianapolis, IN 46278*

# *Trademarks*

*My research into the history of twentieth century computers is dedicated to the memory of my father, Dr. Noonian Soong, and my daughter, Lal.*
—Lt. Commander Data, U.S.S. Enterprise


*This book is dedicated to my brother Mike, who encouraged me to pursue a career in Starfleet, and to my beloved Scott who provided loving support during the creation of this book—in a very special way, these words are as much his as they are mine.*
—Jennifer Flynn, Director of Training and Course Curricula, Starfleet Academy, Earth

# Credits

**Publisher**
*Marie Butler-Knight*

**Associate Publisher**
*Lisa A. Bucki*

**Managing Editor**
*Elizabeth Keaffaber*

**Acquisitions Manager**
*Stephen R. Poland*

**Development Editors**
*Faithe Wempen*
*Mary Cole Rack*

**Manuscript Editor**
*Barry Childs-Helton*

**Cover Designer**
*Tim Amrhein*

**Interior Designer**
*Roger Morgan*

**Indexer**
*Suzanne Snyder*

**Production Team**
*Diana Bigham, Brad Chin, Scott Cook, Tim Cox, Mark Enochs,
Howard Jones, Tom Loveman, Barry Pruett, Beth Rago, Joe Ramon,
Carrie Roth, Dennis Sheehan, Greg Simsic, Mary Beth Wakefield*

*Special thanks to Michael Hanks for ensuring the technical accuracy of this book.*

# Acknowledgements

Both Data and I would like to acknowledge the contributions of our friends and colleagues, without whom this book would not have been possible:

*Of the U.S.S. Enterprise*: Captain Jean-Luc Picard, First Officer William T. Riker, Counselor Deanna Troi, Lieutenant Commander Geordi La Forge, Dr. Beverly Crusher, and Lieutenant Worf.

*Of Starfleet:* Chief of Operations Thomas Loveman, Dr. Leah Brahms, Twentieth Century Earth Historian Michael Hanks, Ensign Wesley Crusher, Lingual Communications Specialist Barry Childs-Helton, Lt. Mary Cole Rack, Lt. Faithe Wempen, Lt. Steve Poland, Lt. Stacy Hiquet, Lt. Commander Lisa Bucki, Lt. Commander Liz Keaffaber, and Commodore Marie Butler-Knight.

*Of the Starfleet Academy of Graphics Communications:* Graphic Specialists Roger Morgan and Scott Cook; Graphic Illustration Specialists: D. F. Scott, Kathy Hanley, and Hans Neuhart.

*Of the Planet Paramount, where extensive Federation histories are kept:* Historian Paula Block—thank you for your patience and your exhaustive research—it meant a lot. From the Advanced Technologies Unit, Dr. Michael Okuda—I can't thank you enough for your technical insights or the hours you put in while "off-duty."

*And to those fellow authors whose works provided me with many hours of enjoyment, insight, and sheer fun:* Larry Nemecek, Michael and Denise Okuda, and Rick Sternbach, among countless others.

*Special thanks to Gene Roddenberry, without whose vision this book would never have existed.*

# Contents

# Preface

I was sitting in my office one day, sipping Bajoran tea, when I received a communication from Lt. Commander Data. I have to admit, it was quite a surprise. It's not as if I hadn't heard of him (I mean, who hasn't heard of the only android in Starfleet?), it's just that I couldn't imagine why he'd be calling me. It seems that Data, like most of us, was in search of his roots. That search led him (naturally enough) to a study of computer development on Earth—concentrating on the twentieth century, when the first digital computers were made. Apparently, with some small amount of encouragement from his friends on board the Enterprise, Data was calling to inquire if I might be interested in looking at his research! Of course I was delighted! With most of the research already completed by Data, I set myself to task. The result is what you now hold in your hands—a supplementary text for the history and computer courses here at Starfleet Academy and abroad, incorporating Data's special insights.

After working with Data for a few months, I got to know him pretty well. So when he proposed that we print the course material on paper and bind it into a book—simply because that's how it was done on twentieth-century Earth—I didn't blink an eye. Perhaps it's a bit eccentric, but what better way for the reader to get a feel for the twentieth century, when books were a great Terran industry and computer technology was in its infancy? Anyway, that's why you're holding this material in your hands, instead of reading it from a screen.

Before you begin this course, let me tell you something else about Lt. Commander Data. First and foremost, he is intensely curious about everything—no detail is too small to go unnoticed. So, if you're a curious person too, I think you'll find this course a remarkable and complete look at how those early computers of Earth actually worked—before the invention of isolinear chips and nanoprocessor units.

Jennifer Flynn
Director of Training and Course Curricula
Starfleet Academy
Earth

Isolinear transcripts available upon request.

# Foreword

*Since my activation on the planet Omicron Theta, I have been curious about my origins. My creator/father, Dr. Noonian Soong, was a reclusive scientist who developed his android technology in almost complete isolation, so there is not very much information about him in the Federation's databanks. I have been told that it is a natural tendency among all beings to search for the answers to the questions, "Who am I?" and "What am I doing here?"*

*It was not until I met my father that I received the answers to even some of my questions. Since his death, I have become interested in the development of computer technology on Earth, the planet of his birth. When my commanding officer, Captain Jean-Luc Picard, suggested that I share my research with Starfleet Academy, I immediately contacted Jennifer Flynn, Director of Training and Course Curricula. What you are reading now is the result of her hard work.*

*I have not yet found the answers to the questions of my existence, but I know that I will continue searching—after all, it is the human thing to do.*

*—Lt. Commander Data, Operations Manager, U.S.S. Enterprise*

# A Guide to This Supplement

*This book is intended to supplement the basic training in computers and Earth history that you will receive at Starfleet Academy. You should read this text after you have completed course number 1200340-C, Computer Technology I, and course number 1345835-H, The History of the Federation, Earth, 1900 to 2200 A.D.*

## Organization

This book is divided into these sections:

- The evolution of computers, from mechanical gears and pulleys to silicon-based microchips, is covered in the *Introduction*.

- The inner workings of the personal computer, and how information was processed, is explored in *Chapters 1 through 6*.

- Methods employed for transferring data between PCs are examined in *Chapters 7 and 8*.

- The separate role of the operating system and software is defined in *Chapter 9*.

- The emerging technologies of the day—including cybernetics, artificial intelligence, fuzzy logic, neural networking, artificial life, the use of fractals in virtual reality, morphing, chaos, and nanotechnology—are explored in *Chapter 10*.

Complete the sections in any order you wish.

# A Personal Note From the Director of Training and Course Curricula

Throughout my career within Starfleet, I have had the privilege of working with many talented beings, many of whom have contributed their insights to this history. I have included their comments throughout the text, but permit me to introduce you to each of the contributing authors now:

*Lt. Commander Data*
*Operations Manager, U.S.S. Enterprise*

Lt. Commander Data made history when he was accepted into the Academy in 2341. As the first android to enter Starfleet, Data has received considerable notoriety—but I think he would give it all up for one day as a "human." His intimate knowledge of computers and how they work helped me to write understandable descriptions of the inner workings of twentieth-century computers. I owe him many thanks.

*Captain Jean-Luc Picard*
*Commanding Officer, U.S.S Enterprise*

Jean-Luc Picard is, in my humble estimation, one of the most interesting captains in Starfleet—he's a diplomat, a poet, a statesman, and an explorer. But it was the Captain's passion for archeology that provided me with valuable insights into the lives of twentieth-century computer users.

*Commander William T. Riker*
*Executive Officer, U.S.S. Enterprise*

Commander Riker possesses an insight which cuts through trivia to reveal truth. His comments reflect his unique perspective on life, computers, and everything in-between.

*Lt. Commander Geordi La Forge*
*Chief of Engineering, U.S.S. Enterprise*

Blind since birth, the Lieutenant Commander "sees" more than just what his VISOR tells him. He has a wonderful talent for explaining complex concepts in simple terms. He spent many hours explaining to me the inner workings of the computer cores on the Enterprise, and for that I'm grateful.

*Dr. Beverly Crusher*
*Chief Medical Officer, U.S.S. Enterprise*

I was a friend of Jack Crusher during his days here at the Academy, and I was thrilled the day he brought me to meet "his Beverly." Beverly's intelligence and versatility have made her indispensable aboard the Starfleet flagship. Her experience with techno-injuries helped me to clarify some questions I had about early computer interaction.

*Lt. Commander Deanna Troi*
*Counselor, U.S.S. Enterprise*

As an expert on human behavior, Counselor Troi helped me to capture the feeling of working with those early PCs. She does not necessarily care *how* a thing worked; instead, her questions addressed such issues as, "*Why* would someone want it to work that way?" and "What was it like to use a keyboard (or modem, or printer)?" I found her perceptions to be most helpful.

*Lieutenant Worf*
*Chief of Security, U.S.S. Enterprise*

Lieutenant Worf, like Data, was also a first: the first Klingon to serve in Starfleet. As Chief of Security aboard the *Enterprise*, Worf was able to assist me in my explanations of security methods used in early PCs.

*Ensign Wesley Crusher*
*Cadet, Starfleet Academy*

I met Wesley during his first year at the Academy, and I found him to be an intriguing contrast: the intelligence and insight of an adult, combined with youthful enthusiasm and curiousity. He recounted many interesting experiences of his time on board the *Enterprise*, most of which I found "illustrative," so I have included them throughout the text.

Look for comments from each of these experts (and some "surprise" guests) throughout the text. To help you relate quickly to the operation of these ancient machines, comparisons to Starship computers are included in special boxes. In addition, there is a complete starship computer reference at the back of this book.

Jennifer Flynn
Director of Training and Curricula
Starfleet Academy
Earth

**Introduction**

# The History of Computers in the Twentieth Century

*Starfleet sociologists concluded long ago that humanioid species cannot acquire the intelligence level required to coexist with the majority of other species until they have invented the computer. By the reckoning of Earth's Old Free World, the electronic computer was invented during the first half of the 1900s though curiously, much of the technology necessary to build a computer was actually invented some three hundred years earlier. Leaders of the planet's individual subcultures apparently overlooked the potential importance of the device until after Earth's second global conflict.*

*—Lt. Commander Data, Operations Manager, U.S.S. Enterprise*

To put Earth's twentieth-century computers in their proper perspective, it is important to understand the technological achievements leading up to that time. In 1642, the French mathematician Blaise *Pascal* invented the first automatic mechanical calculator, called the *Pascaline*. It could only perform addition and subtraction, and its gears had to be turned by hand, but it was the start of a long line of mechanical calculators constructed with gears and pulleys.

Pascal was later honored for his historic achievements when, in the early 1970s, Dr. Niklaus Wirth named his programming language "Pascal."

In 1804, another Frenchman, Joseph-Marie *Jacquard* programmed a weaving loom that utilized a series of punched cards to form patterns in the woven fabric. This inspired a series of computers (even well into the twentieth century) that accepted their data on punched cards or tape.

*I wonder, since these early computers were built entirely of gears and pulleys, if this is the origin of the term "to crank out an answer?"*
**—Lt. Commander Data, Operations Manager, U.S.S. Enterprise**

The Englishman Charles *Babbage* (the grandfather of the first true Terran computers) constructed his *Difference Engine*—a large mechanical calculator capable of addition and subtraction in 1822. In his later years, Babbage designed an *Analytical Engine*—which was to be a general-purpose calculation machine. Though never built, its basic

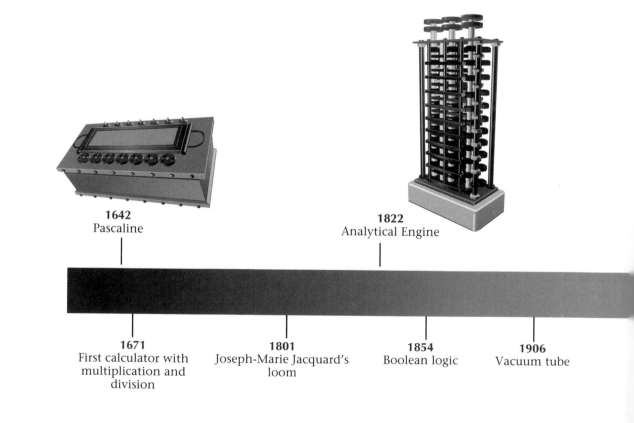

**1642**
Pascaline

**1822**
Analytical Engine

**1671**
First calculator with multiplication and division

**1801**
Joseph-Marie Jacquard's loom

**1854**
Boolean logic

**1906**
Vacuum tube

design has fundamental similarities to later computers, even those in use today.

In 1854, the British mathematican George S. *Boole* formulated a method for representing logic through mathematical formulas. He was working to prove a theory that combinations of these principal formulas comprised all intelligent human thought. His theory was never proven, though the scope of his achievement was at last realized in 1946, when it was discovered that *transistors* could be used to represent and execute Boolean logic electronically.

# Enter the Twentieth Century

Early in the century, the *vacuum tube* was invented; however, its application to computers was not exploited until the late 1930s.

The first computers built in the twentieth century were still partly mechanical, typically constructed from a combination of counting wheels and electromagnetic relays, recieving input from punched tape.

In 1939, John Vincent *Anatasoff* and his assistant, Clifford *Berry*, built the first computer to use vacuum tubes. It is important to note that these early computers were almost all single-purpose calculating machines. For example, one of the first computers ever constructed was designed for the single purpose of calculating mathematical tables. A few years later, in Germany, the first programmable computer was built. It was constructed with vacuum tubes (electronic computers were still a few years away), and it received its instructions from a piece of punched photographic film. A similar computer, called the Mark I, was built in America a few years later. The Mark I project

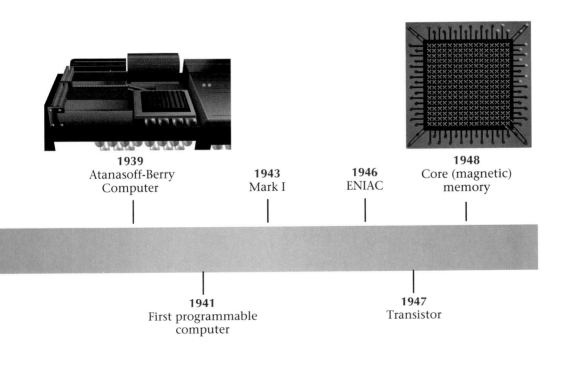

**1939**
Atanasoff-Berry
Computer

**1943**
Mark I

**1946**
ENIAC

**1948**
Core (magnetic)
memory

**1941**
First programmable
computer

**1947**
Transistor

was noteworthy because one of its collaborators was a company called *IBM* (International Business Machines).

Not only were vacuum-tube computers greatly limited in their potential purpose, but they were also quite large compared to later electronic versions. In order to improve the computing capacity of computers made with vacuum tubes, larger and larger computers were constructed. Eventually they occupied whole floors of buildings. It was not until the development of *ENIAC* (Electronic Numerical Integrator And Computer) in 1946 that a general-purpose electonic digital computer attained a manageable size.

ENIAC was originally designed to calculate missle trajectories for the American army during Earth's Second World War, but it was completed too late. Its general-purpose design, however, allowed it to be used for other tasks, including scientific calculation. ENIAC was built using approximately 18,000 vacuum tubes. One reason for the large amount of tubes was that ENIAC used a decimal storage system, instead of the *binary* system used today. Instructing the earliest computers (such as ENIAC) to perform a task was tedious, because they had to be programmed manually. In 1946, the Austrian physicist John *von Neumann* designed the first electronically-programmable computer.

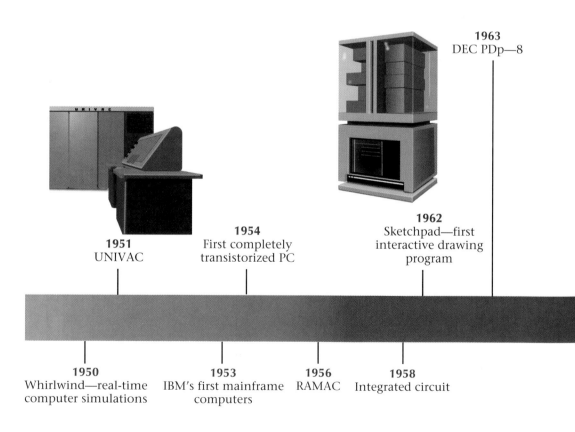

**1963**
DEC PDp—8

**1962**
Sketchpad—first interactive drawing program

**1951**
UNIVAC

**1954**
First completely transistorized PC

**1950**
Whirlwind—real-time computer simulations

**1953**
IBM's first mainframe computers

**1956**
RAMAC

**1958**
Integrated circuit

The word *binary* refers to something which has only two states, such as a light which can only be on or off. The electronic computer of the 1900s stored data by using the binary states of its components. By switching certain components on or off, a pattern could be formed which represented a letter, a decimal number, or the answer to a question.

In a binary (base 2) system, only two digits are used[md]1 and 0. Each "place" represents a factor of 2. For example, the first row of tubes would represent $2^0$ or just 0, the second row would represent $2^1$ (2x1), the third row would represent 4 (2x2), the fourth row 8 (2x2x2), and so on. In a binary system, a single tube could be used to represent 1 when on, and 0 when off. The decimal number 46 equals 101110 in base 2, or (2x2x2x2x2) + (2x2x2) + (2x2) + 2 or 32+8+4+2 or 46. Here is how the number 46 would look in such a system:

| Tube | status |
|------|--------|
| **Row 1** | On |
| **Row 2** | Off |
| **Row 3** | On |
| **Row 4** | On |
| **Row 5** | On |
| **Row 6** | Off |

Even with such a small number, the savings were perceived as enormous: a mere 6 tubes, as opposed to 20.

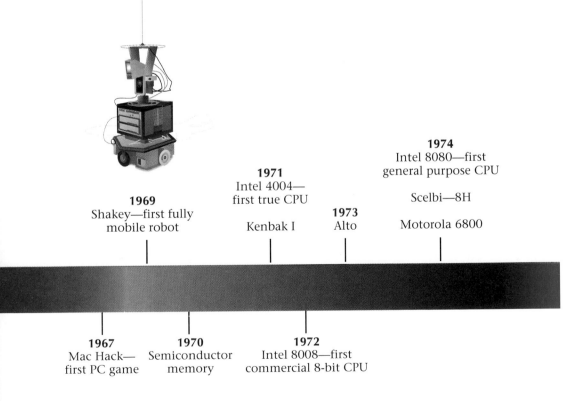

**1969**
Shakey—first fully
mobile robot

**1971**
Intel 4004—
first true CPU

Kenbak I

**1973**
Alto

**1974**
Intel 8080—first
general purpose CPU

Scelbi—8H

Motorola 6800

**1967**
Mac Hack—
first PC game

**1970**
Semiconductor
memory

**1972**
Intel 8008—first
commercial 8-bit CPU

# From Vacuum Tubes to Microchips

At first, computers were built only on special commission for a subcultural government, either for the purpose of conducting warfare or defense operations. Once it became feasible to design and manufacture multi-purpose computers, they were sold in large quantities, mainly to universities and learning institutions. The *UNIVAC* (**Uni**versal **A**utomatic **C**omputer) was the first computer to be successfully sold commercially. UNIVAC used memory that was composed of mercury-filled acoustic delay lines, and it stored data on magnetic tape.

Gradually computers evolved from single-purpose to general-purpose, but they still retained their large size. In 1949, a means of recording data magnetically (*core memory*) replaced vacuum tubes as a more reliable form of memory storage. In 1956, the first computer to utilize magnetic storage, *RAMAC,* was built.

The invention of the *integrated circuit* in 1958 led to smaller and smaller computers, until they eventually fit in the palm of a Terran hand. But this "downsizing" of com-

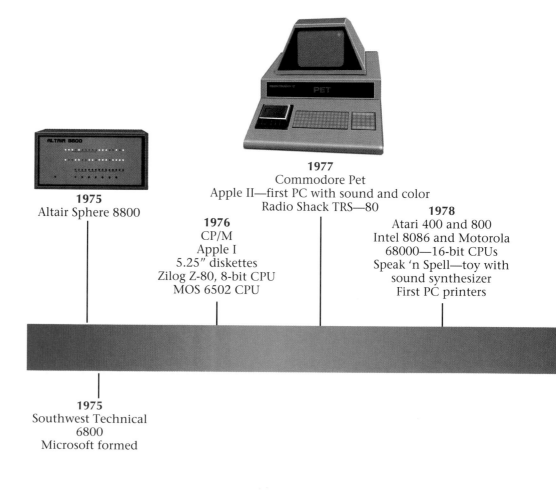

**1975**
Altair Sphere 8800

**1977**
Commodore Pet
Apple II—first PC with sound and color
Radio Shack TRS—80

**1976**
CP/M
Apple I
5.25" diskettes
Zilog Z-80, 8-bit CPU
MOS 6502 CPU

**1978**
Atari 400 and 800
Intel 8086 and Motorola
68000—16-bit CPUs
Speak 'n Spell—toy with
sound synthesizer
First PC printers

**1975**
Southwest Technical
6800
Microsoft formed

puters did not happen overnight. Large computers called *mainframes* dominated until the mid-1960s, when slightly smaller computers of a similar design (called *mini-computers*) were introduced. Digital Equipment Corporation, the leading manufacturer of mini-computers, introduced its first model, the *PDP-8* "Programmed Data Processor," in 1963. These mainframes and mini-computers processed data from central cores similar in concept to the ones we use on starships today. *Centralized processing*, as it was called, was the norm until personal computers were introduced in the mid-1970s.

The *personal computer* (*PC*) was first seen as a toy for electronic hobbyists; its true significance was not understood until years later. Several PCs were created around the same time, including the Kenbak I, Scelbi-8H, Sphere 1, KIM-1, South West Technical PC, Sol/8, and the Xerox Alto, but none of these matched the commercial success of the

Altair 8800—because of its success, in most histories the Altair 8800 was given the honor of "first personal computer." By the end of the century, personal computers were commonplace; it was not unusual to find a computer in most homes.

In the mid-1970s on Earth, there was a revolution going on. The personal computer was beginning to become a popular computing tool and not just a hobby, so soon everyone was (as a common phrase went) "jumping on the bandwagon." Many companies started producing personal computers, but very few of them survived for more than a year. One company, Apple Computers, survived by selling computers with an operating scheme completely different from that used in most PCs of the time. These were the Apple II and Macintosh computers. The Macintosh series employed the first popular system for *arranging visual data graphically* as stylized pictures; it was originally called the "Finder." Later incorporated into the overall Apple System, Finder was the first product in a category called *graphical user interfaces (GUI)*.

**1979**
Intel 8088
CompuServe
Hayes modems
Speechlab, voice recognition
Visicalc, first spreadsheet
WordStar

**1980**
First 32 bit CPU
Sinclair ZX 80, first PC
exclusively for home
Color monitors

**1981**
MS-DOS
Osborne, first "laptop" PC
First color printer
Hayes Smartmodem 300

> *It is unclear from our history files exactly what a "bandwagon" was, and whether it was used for musical performance or transportation, but we do know that in times of excitement, people of the twentieth century often liked to jump onto it.*
> **—Lt. Commander Data, Operations Manager, U.S.S. Enterprise**

A graphical user interface (GUI) incorporated pictures (called *icons*) and *menus* (organized lists of available commands) that made learning to use the computer much easier than before. Many earlier computers had used a basic *command-line interface* popularized by the most widely-distributed operating system of the day, MS-DOS (**M**icrosoft **d**isk **o**perating **s**ystem). With a command-line interface, the user typed words (or specific abbreviated commands that had to be memorized). These appeared on the screen beside a a *prompt*, a blinking horizontal line that indicated DOS was ready to accept a command.

The Macintosh was not actually the first PC to use a graphical user interface. Early experiments by Xerox Corporation in the use of a mouse-controlled computer called Alto led to the formal introduction of GUIs to the outside world. The Xerox Star, as it was called, was moderately successful, though it failed to gain widespread acceptance. Many of its designers left Xerox to design the Apple Lisa. The Lisa was the first PC to feature both a graphical user interface and *integrated software* as standard equipment. The Lisa gained

**1981**
IBM PC

**1982**
3.5" diskettes
Lotus 1-2-3
Intel 286
Commodore 64
First notebook PC
Computer is Time Magazine's
"Man of the Year"

widespread acclaim—though not widespread acceptance, because it was too expensive and slow compared to command-line PCs such as the IBM PC. The creators of the Lisa did not stop trying to commercialize the GUI concept—Apple Chairman Steven Jobs followed their Lisa PC with the highly successful Macintosh PC.

The operating system of a PC controls the processing of information and handles program requests, much like our own LCARS (Library Computer Access and Retrieval System). You'll learn more about the role of operating systems such as MS-DOS in Chapter 9.

# The Development of PC Standards

As great as Apple was, it was another company, IBM (International Business Machines) that developed the computer that would eventually become the standard. IBM coined the widespread use of the term "PC" by adopting it as a brandname. After IBM introduced its first PC in 1981, its immense popularity—coupled with a surprising lack of design patents—compelled most of the computer manufacturers to follow its design. MS-DOS was adopted as standard because IBM shipped it with IBM PCs as their "native" operating system. MS-DOS was therefore easy to regard as an integral part of the PC. For this reason, authors of programs for the PC came to write their software to run under

**1983**
IBM X/T
Lisa
Androbot, robots
for the home
Novell

**1984**
Macintosh
IBM A/T
IBM PCjr
WordPerfect
Virtual reality studies
HP LaserJet—first laser printer

**1985**
CD ROMs
Artificial intelligence studies
Intel 386
Windows 1.0

MS-DOS. It meant the demise of other viable operating systems (such as Digital Research's CP/M).

Apple/Macintosh maintained its own operating system, and continued to service a specialized market: computer graphics and electronic publishing. The persistence of the Apple/Macintosh graphical user interface led to the creation of "friendlier" operating systems for the MS-DOS-compatible machines. These included Windows and OS/2, with MS-DOS itself eventually disappearing.

Challengers to the MS-DOS operating system appeared in various forms. Digital Research, the creators of the CP/M operating system, came back to challenge MS-DOS in the early 1990s with its DR DOS. Although DR DOS contained many "user-friendly" features that MS-DOS did not contain, Microsoft had an advantage. Its exclusive

distribution agreements with computer manufacturers led to MS-DOS being sold to customers without their expressly choosing it. DR was unable to obtain such exclusive agreements, making MS-DOS difficult to unseat. Microsoft was not the only company to benefit from close identification with the first IBM PC. Another company, Intel, also profited when its microprocessor, the Intel 8088, was chosen as the microprocessor for the IBM PC.

Microsoft Windows—first a GUI add-on interface for MS-DOS and later an operating system in its own right—brought GUIs to the masses. An alternative to Windows called OS/2 was later introduced by IBM. Unlike Windows (which started as an add-on environment), OS/2 was a complete *replacement* for MS-DOS. Like Windows, OS/2 allowed *multitasking* (the processing of more than a

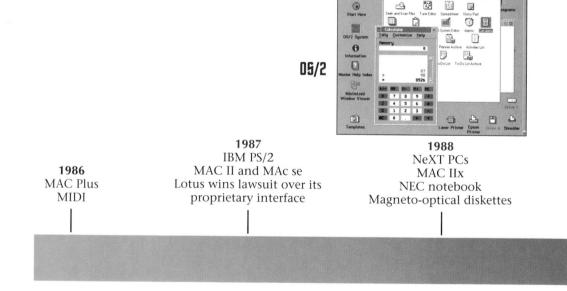

OS/2

**1986**
MAC Plus
MIDI

**1987**
IBM PS/2
MAC II and MAc se
Lotus wins lawsuit over its
proprietary interface

**1988**
NeXT PCs
MAC IIx
NEC notebook
Magneto-optical diskettes

single program at a time). In this era, multitasking was a special feature of operating systems, and not a standard feature of personal computers. OS/2, because of its adherence to IBM's SAA (**S**ystem **A**pplication **A**rchitecture) standards, was compatible with a wide range of computer platforms—from mainframes to mini-computers to PCs. OS/2 proved a formidable challenge to Microsoft Windows.

An alternative computer, the NeXT PC, utilized an operating system which featured a graphical user interface, *high-resolution graphics* (a clearer, sharper screen image), and digital sound processing. NeXT Computers was founded by Steven Jobs, a former co-founder of Apple Computers. Like the Apple, the NeXT PC was ahead of its time, but found limited success as a replacement for UNIX-based PCs. (You'll learn more about operating systems such as UNIX in Chapter 9.)

Both Microsoft and Intel continued to influence the design of computers well beyond the twentieth century. By the 1990s, Microsoft was Earth's leading manufacturer of computer *software*, the term for the products of this new industry. The products were programs—known commercially as *applications*—that instructed the computer to perform specific tasks. These included word processing, database management, time management, and sales analysis. When a user wanted their PC to perform some new task, they would purchase a specific software program to instruct the computer on how to perform it. As a leader in software development, Microsoft influenced *how computers were used*.

Intel continued to manufacture microprocessors into the twenty-second century, when microprocessors were replaced by nanoprocessors. Nanoprocessors are used throughout the Federation, within most computers. Nanoprocessors take some of the processing load from the central core, speeding access times. You'll learn more about processors in Chapter 2.

**1989**
EISA bus architecture
Apple SE/30
MS-DOS 4.0
GRidPad, handwriting
recognition system
MAC IIci
Intel 486

**1990**
Windows 3.0
Multimedia
Pen based PCs
IBM's PS/1
Bell Labs invents the
optical microprocessor

**1991**
IBM invents the
single atom switch

IBM was a leading manufacturer of computers on Earth in the twentieth century. The company's progenitor, the Computing-Tabulating-Recording Company, had specialized in mechanical tabulating machines since 1911. After IBM's success with the Mark I, the company began manufacturing large computers (called *mainframes*) for business. Later, IBM led the world in the manufacture of personal computers (PCs). Although it was difficult for any one company to dominate the diverse personal computer market, IBM was very influential, for reasons that were partly intentional, and partly accidental. IBM suffered some setbacks in the early 1990s. Its firm foundation, however—as one of the most well-structured corporations ever formed—helped the corporation not only to survive, but to flourish well into the twenty-fourth century. In the late 2060's, IBM returned to its concentration on central mainframe-like computers, manufacturing the GL1000 series, the HAL 2001, the computers at Memory Alpha 1, and the first central cores used in starships. These were many orders of magnitude more efficient and powerful than their predecessors.

As a Betazoid and a counselor on the Starship Enterprise, my expertise is in people, not computers. So I was a bit surprised when Data asked me if I would contribute something to this course. But one of the most fascinating things about the study of the early Terran personal computers is (at least, for me) not how they worked, but how they were used. For example, personal computers were the most visible form of computers in the twentieth century—but they were by no means the only type in use. When we think back to that part of history, we generally forget that computers had, in the course of a few decades, invaded the everyday life of the people of Earth in many ways.

Computers were used to automate communications, transportation, entertainment, and sometimes the home itself. For example, the best homes were often equipped with a computerized system that regulated lighting, temperature, and security in a way that was more energy-efficient and convenient than the manual system most people employed. These environmental computers became the forebears of the environmental controls we use aboard starships today.

—*Counselor Deanna Troi,*
*U.S.S. Enterprise*

**Windows 3.1**

**1992**
Windows 3.1
Intel 486
MS-DOS 5.0
OS/2 v2.0
Apple System 7

**1993**
Pentium

**1994**
Windows NT

# Chapter One

# Tracing the Path of the Letter D

On the surface, the ability to give verbal commands to the ship's computer seems more convenient than the ancient practice of typing commands on a keyboard, or selecting them with a pointing device. But I can tell you from experience that providing the right input using only verbal commands is sometimes far from easy. I once had a sort of "living nightmare" where all my friends and colleagues were somehow disappearing one by one. Soon, my only companion was the computer, and after long hours of frustration, I stumbled upon an answer by finally asking the computer the "right" questions. My friends had not disappeared; I was trapped in a collapsing static warp bubble. Once I understood the situation, I was able to ask more "right" questions and find a way out before the bubble disappeared with me in it. It was a very frustrating and humbling experience, but remembering it always reminds me of how important "the right question" is.

—*Doctor Beverly Crusher, Chief Medical Officer, U.S.S. Enterprise*

In the late twentieth century, most everyday computing tasks on Earth were performed on individual, self-contained units known as "personal computers" (PCs). While Federation computers are designed to meet the simultaneous needs of thousands, the twentieth-century PC was designed for a single user. Even so, these primitive systems processed, displayed, and stored information with remarkable ingenuity.

The heart of the PC was the *system unit*, which housed the main components of the PC itself. Located within the system unit was the *CPU*, which processed information; *memory*, which held that information temporarily while it was being processed; and the *hard disk*, which stored the information after it was processed. Also located within the system unit was *ROM*, which held the permanent instructions needed for handling the PC's most basic functions.

The PC consisted of two other components besides the system unit: a *monitor* on which a PC displayed information, and a *keyboard* through which the user entered commands. In later chapters, you will learn about the inner workings of each PC component. In this chapter, you will start at the beginning of your PC odyssey by learning how commands were issued to the PC through its keyboard.

In the Federation, we have become accustomed to built-in convenience—Federation computers accept both voice and keypad input; Betazoid computers even accept telepathic input. But a twentieth-century PC received most of its data and commands through its keyboard, which had been developed from still more ancient writing machines. Unlike the touch-sensitive surfaces of control panels in Federation computers, early keyboards required the user to actually press and release individual mechanical keys. To minimize mistakes, the user was obliged to learn how to "type," a complex technique for pressing the keys in sequence to spell out entire words. Because the keyboard was mechanical in nature, issuing commands to the computer was a noisy and laborious process by present day standards.

Compare this process with the method used to enter commands through a control panel of a Federation computer—in which keypads represent particular functions, and touching

*The control panels of the Enterprise can be reprogrammed for any function.*

a symbol performs a task (such as launching a probe). The process used for entering commands to Starfleet computers is mostly *symbolic*—a logical choice which enables them to be used by crew members from many different cultures. Twentieth-century computers, however, used a command process that was mostly *linguistic*. Commands were generally entered as entire words, or as specific key combinations that represented an abbreviated verbal command. For example, to copy documents from one part of permanent storage to another, the user might type **COPY** or press the **Alt** and **C** keys simultaneously.

*Actually, the control panels on board Galaxy-class starships are more sophisticated than you might think. For example, I sat at the Conn while I was an acting ensign on the Enterprise, and from there, I could program the control panel for Ops, or for any other task, such as launching a probe. Depending on the task I programmed it to do, the keypads on the control panel would change (along with their associated function). For example, as I worked at a task, a subprocessor within the control panel constantly updated the keypad display, optimizing the layout for ongoing efficiency. Even if you didn't know a lot about piloting a ship, the control panel could be programmed to "teach" you which keys to press by presenting a limited selection.*

**—Ensign Wesley Crusher, Cadet, Starfleet Academy**

The progression of computer input from linguistic to symbolic began on Earth in 1979 at the now famous Palo Alto Research Center (PARC). Xerox, a company involved in the early development of PCs, ran the PARC center. Xerox's first steps into the realm of symbolic user controls (later called a graphical user interface) resulted in a PC they called (appropriately enough) the Alto. Later developments in the graphical user interface resulted in the Xerox Star, Apple Lisa, and still later, the entire series of Apple Macintosh computers.

Graphical user interfaces (GUIs) incorporated two-dimensional symbols (called *icons*) that represented specific tasks or programs. These symbols were usually small pictures, often labeled with words so the user could easily ascertain their purpose. By manipulating these icons on-screen with a device called a mouse, the user could invoke various commands.

However, the most popular PCs of the twentieth century, the IBM compatibles, did not use a symbolic operating system. They depended instead on linguistic input—words typed at a prompt. Graphical user interfaces were later incorporated into the IBM compatible PCs as a processing layer on top of the operating system. Because they created entire "environments" of pictures and words, these programs were called *operating environments*. Popular operating environments for IBM compatibles included Microsoft Windows, OS/2 Presentation Manager, and GeoWorks. But although these operating environments were a step in the direction of symbolic input, they were not a complete step. Operating environments, in order to be compatible with programs designed for the IBM compatibles, still had to be able to accept linguistic input in the form of typed commands, or words selected from the screen. You'll learn more about the role of the PC's operating system, and also of operating environments in Chapter 9.

3

# Storing the Press of a Key

Because twentieth century PCs were mostly linguistic in nature, the user had to enter commands at the keyboard by pressing certain keys in sequence. To understand the steps it took for such a PC to process a single "keypress," you will follow its path through the PC's inner workings.

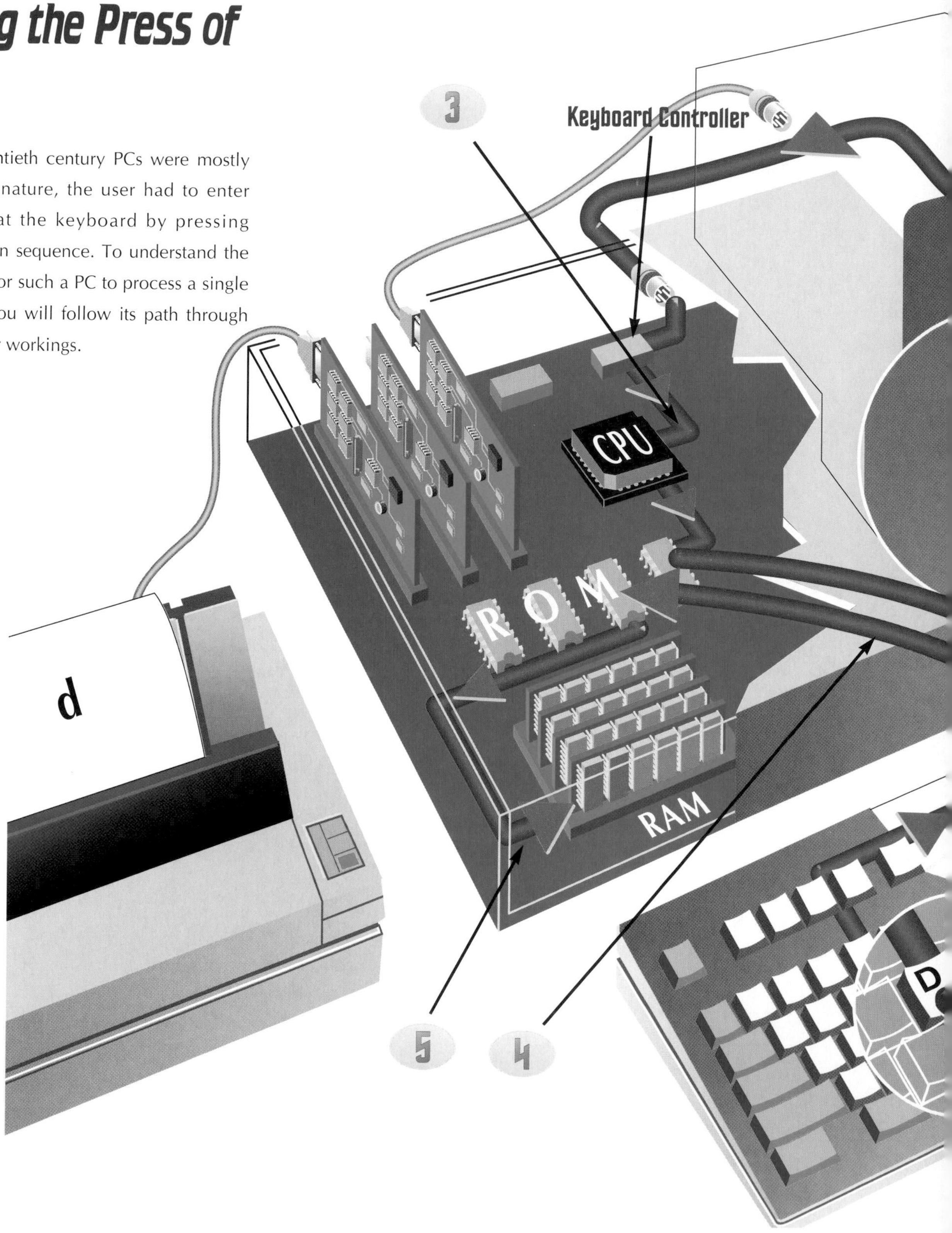

**3**

**Keyboard Controller**

CPU

ROM

RAM

**5**

**4**

d

D

4

1. When the user pressed a key (such as the lowercase **d** key), an electrical circuit was completed. Because the keyboard's CPU was constantly scanning the circuits leading to all the keys, the change in current was noticed almost immediately.

2. Every key on the keyboard was associated with a particular set of codes, called *scan codes*. When a key was pressed, the appropriate codes were determined, and then these codes were stored temporarily in a special chip called the *keyboard buffer*.

3. After the codes were safely stored, the keyboard CPU sent a signal to the *keyboard controller* chip inside the system unit, notifying it that a key had been pressed. The keyboard controller responded to this signal by sending an *interrupt* to the CPU (**c**entral **p**rocessing **u**nit). The CPU performed all of the PC's calculations and analyses, while occasionally delegating certain tasks to other components.

An *interrupt* was a signal to the CPU that indicated a particular device needed the CPU's exclusive attention for a short period. When the CPU received an interrupt, it stored what it was working on, and immediately answered the call. Interrupts were issued whenever input or output was required: for example, the press of a key, the movement of a mouse, or the display of information on the monitor.

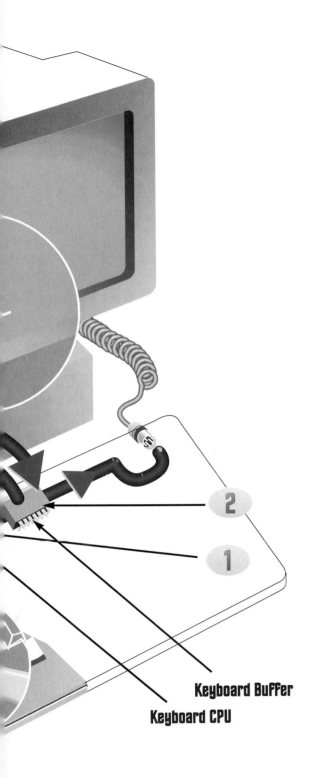

**Keyboard Buffer**

**Keyboard CPU**

*The two scan codes included the make code, which indicated the pressing of a key, and the break code, which indicated its release.*

4. The CPU would then stop its current task, and instruct the ROM BIOS (**B**asic **I**nput **O**utput **S**ystem) to take the appropriate action. In response to this particular interrupt, ROM BIOS retrieved the scan codes from the keyboard buffer chip, and translated the codes into ASCII.

5. Once ROM converted the scan code for the **d** key to a two-byte value, that value was stored in a special area in RAM called the *keyboard buffer*. (This "keyboard buffer" was different from the "keyboard buffer" mentioned earlier; the first buffer was a chip within the keyboard which stored scan codes for keys as they were pressed, until the time when those codes were transferred to the keyboard controller inside the system unit. The keyboard buffer referred to here was a logical area of RAM where keypresses were stored as two-byte values, ready for processing by a program.) If any program needed to know which key(s) were being pressed, it issued an interrupt to request that the keyboard data be passed from the keyboard buffer (the area of RAM) to the program.

*Some keys (such as the function keys, or the arrow keys) had no ASCII equivalent, so other codes were used instead.*

ASCII (**A**merican **S**tandard **C**ode for **I**nformation **I**nterchange) was a standard table of binary codes used by all PCs. Although there was only one **d** key on the keyboard, there were two ASCII codes for that key: one code for a lowercase **d**, and another code for an uppercase **D**. In order for the user to select the intended purpose of a keypress, there were *state-changing keys*. State-changing keys had only one purpose: to change the value associated with other keys. One of these, the Shift key, changed the value of any letter key; when pressed at the same time as the **d** key, for example, the Shift key changed the **d** from lowercase to uppercase **D**. Likewise, if another state-changing key (such as Ctrl or Alt) was pressed with the **d** key, the resulting *key combination* could cause a program to perform some specific task, such as saving a file for later use.

If the user pressed a state-changing key (**Shift**, **Ctrl**, or **Alt**), a special *flag* (a two-byte code) was stored in RAM (memory—the area within the PC where data was stored temporarily as it was processed). While translating a scan code, ROM BIOS checked this area of memory, and used what it found there to change the two-byte value it was calculating. ROM calculated a specific two-byte value if the **d** key had been pressed alone; it calculated *different* two-byte values if it found the **d** key had been pressed in combination with Shift, Alt, or Ctrl.

In addition, as ROM translated a scan code, it watched for specific key combinations. One of these—**Ctrl** and **Alt** and **Delete**, signaled the computer to stop what it was doing and *reboot* (restart by reloading the operating system). When ROM recognized that these three keys had been pressed simultaneously, it would automatically run the reboot routine.

*Progression from a strictly linguistic interface to other forms of input is a natural progression in the development of computers on many worlds. The next logical step in the development of Federation computers is a tighter symbiosis between the user and the machine. When I last visited the Enterprise, I found young Wesley Crusher to be quite adept at "connecting" with the computer, as we worked together to rescue his mother from a collapsing warp bubble. In all, an encouraging sign for the members of the Federation.*

*—The Traveler*

*The Traveler is one of a few beings who can achieve a true symbiosis between user and machine.*

# Displaying a Key Press

1. To display the letter **d** on the screen, a program issued a software interrupt (a signal for the CPU's attention). The CPU would then signal ROM BIOS to run the appropriate interrupt routine.

2. ROM BIOS moved the scan code from the keyboard buffer in RAM to one of the CPU's *registers* (high-speed memory area inside the CPU chip).

3. Next, the program computed the location at which it wanted to display the letter **d** on the monitor screen. After the location was calculated, the program issued an instruction to the CPU to move the contents of the CPU register. The code for the letter **d** was then moved to the location within *video* memory that had been calculated by the program. (Video memory was an area of RAM which contained the data currently being displayed on the monitor.)

4. The video controller constantly read video memory, and it noticed when the contents of video memory had changed.

5. The video controller added control signals to the display data which the monitor's electron guns used to refresh (redraw) the screen image. This action placed the letter **d** on the screen. This entire sequence took only a fraction of a second. It was then repeated for the next letter or symbol to be displayed.

Twentieth-century computer displays were actually simple electromechanical devices. Data being displayed were encoded as signals that were sent through an electron beam called a *cathode ray*. This electron beam would strike the inside of the monitor's screen, which was coated with a phosphorescent substance that produced light when struck by the beam. The image formed by this light created the image on the display. Early computer monitors were the sole analog electrical device in PCs, which were otherwise entirely digital in nature and design.

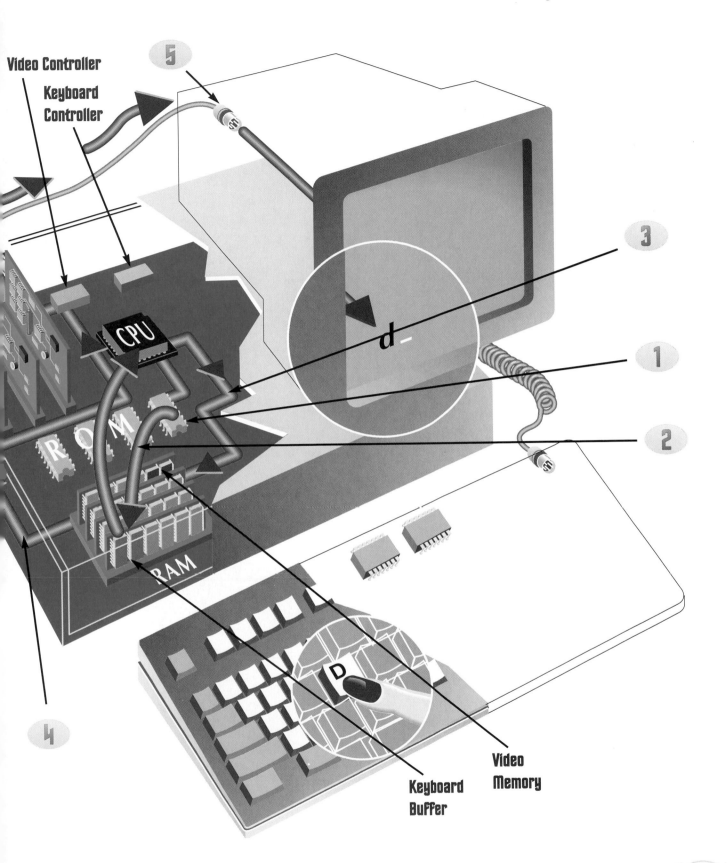

Video Controller

Keyboard
Controller

CPU

ROM

RAM

d_

D

Keyboard
Buffer

Video
Memory

5

3

1

2

4

# Printing a Key Press

If a program's task was to print the letter **d** on *hard copy* (paper), the program would again send a software interrupt to the CPU. The CPU would request ROM BIOS to handle the interrupt, a ROM BIOS would in turn move the pattern for the letter **d** to a portion of the computer called a *port*. Like a passenger awaiting travel at a spaceport, a character sent to a port awaited passage through a *data interface* (*cable*) to the *printer*. A printer was a mechanical device which translated digital signals from the PC into electrical signals which caused it to apply inks or other pigments in specific patterns to paper. You will learn more about the workings of a printer and the specifics of ink transfer in later chapters.

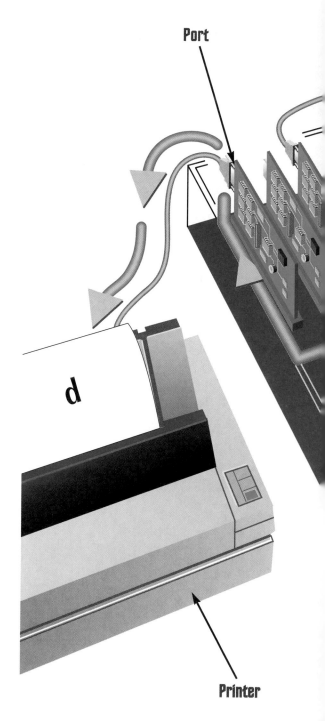

**Port**

**d**

**Printer**

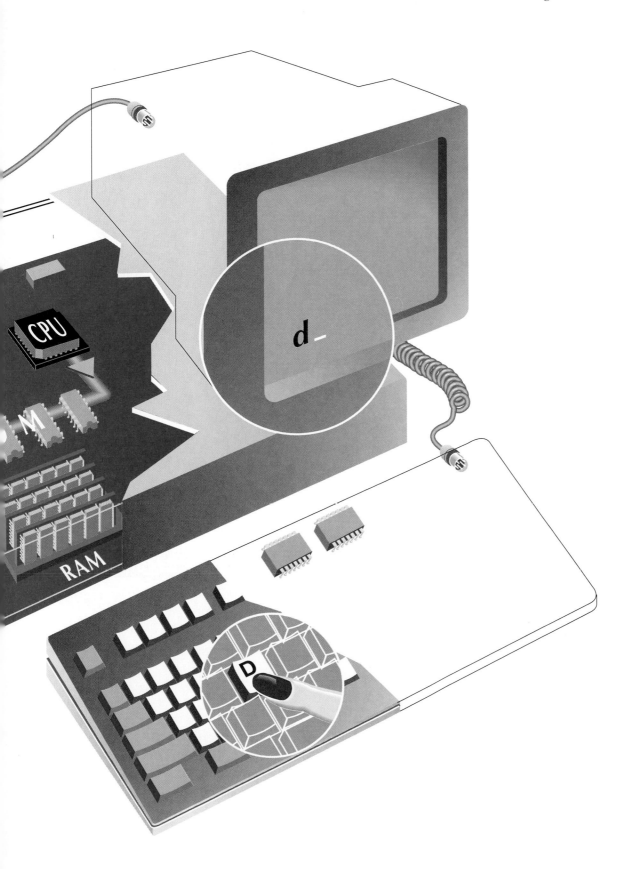

Although it is now commonplace to store data on isolinear chips, older methods of preserving information still have their place. On Earth, *paper* was the most popular storage medium of the twentieth century, though invented thousands of years earlier. However, due to harsh acids used in the paper-making process of the 1900s, very little has survived. It was created from plant fibers (usually wood) laid down on a fine screen from a water suspension; when dried, this substance formed a solid surface upon which letters and numbers could be written. The book you are reading was created using these ancient methods, to demonstrate the continuing usefulness of hard copy. For example, if you were outdoors on the day side of a Class M planet (or near a window), you could still read this book in the event of a power loss; if you were in orbit—even if your ship's computers were being upgraded—you would need only a source of artificial illumination.

*When I think of what the people of twentieth century Earth had to go through just to issue a command to one of their computers, I wonder how it was possible to get anything done while using them. Betazoid computers are much more sensible (unlike men); all I have to do is think the command, and it's done. I'm astonished that more computers are not designed this way. But of course, they had to start somewhere.*

—Lwaxana Troi,
Betazed Ambassador,
Daughter of the Fifth House,
Holder of the Sacred Chalice of Reaks,
and Heir to the Holy Rings of Betazed.

**Chapter**            **Two**

# The Core of the Personal Computer: The System Unit

Compared to the computer technologies now in use throughout the Federation, on Earth the workings of a typical twentieth-century personal computer were simple. A basic PC system had three components: the keyboard was used to enter commands and data—you had to press its keys in sequence; the monitor displayed information on an old-style vacuum tube; the system unit housed the main components of the computer itself. The typical user had only a vague idea of what went on inside a PC because there was little need to know more; PCs, like the computers in use today, were dependable, well-engineered machines.

—Lt. Commander Geordi La Forge,
Chief of Engineering, U.S.S. Enterprise

Twentieth-century PCs did not have a central control like the Federation's LCARS (Library Computer Access and Retrieval System), so they lacked the flexible system support and data retrieval that Federation computers enjoy. Instead, each PC had its own *operating system* to control basic system activity such as data storage and retrieval, and its own *applications*; these were *programs* that made specific tasks (such as drawing or writing) possible. When the user needed the PC to perform a new task, he or she would purchase an additional application that would instruct the PC to perform that new task. You will learn more about the role of the operating systems and programs later in this course.

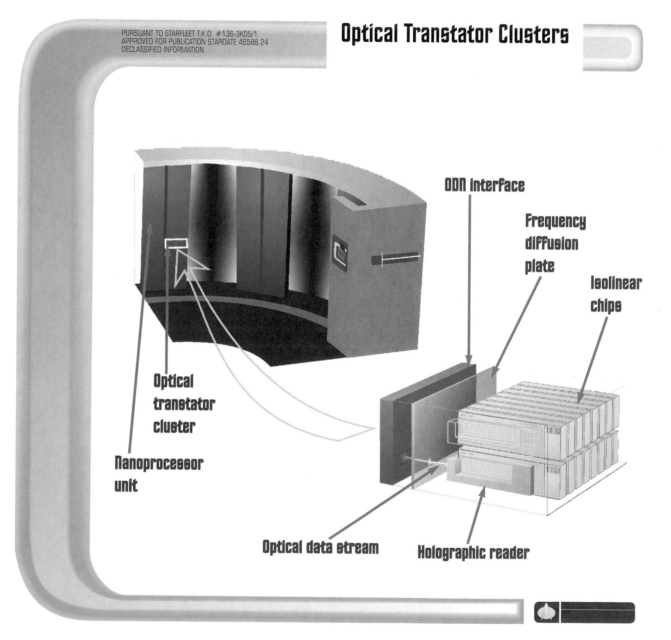

PURSUANT TO STARFLEET T.K.O. #136-3K05/1
APPROVED FOR PUBLICATION STARDATE 46588.24
DECLASSIFIED INFORMATION

## Optical Transtator Clusters

ODN interface

Frequency diffusion plate

Isolinear chips

Optical transtator cluster

Nanoprocessor unit

Optical data stream

Holographic reader

For now, we will turn our concentration to the inner workings of a twentieth century PC. As you learned in the last chapter, the twentieth century PC was comprised of three basic components: the monitor, the keyboard, and the system unit. The monitor was used to display data and the keyboard was used to input commands and data from the user. But it was the inner components of the system unit which processed that data and controlled its input and output. You have already learned how certain PC components—the keyboard, CPU, ROM, and RAM worked together to process keystrokes entered by the user. Keeping that general overview in mind, let's take a closer examination of the system unit and all of its component parts.

The computers on board all *Galaxy* class starships are the sophisticated, complex descendants of the twentieth-century personal computer. The main core of the *Enterprise's* computer, for example, has ten levels (three upper and seven primary). Each level is divided into four modules that house independently functioning nanoprocessor units arranged in logical clusters. A bank of 16 isolinear chips controls each cluster (of which there are 256 per module), and an individual cluster has 1,024 segments—an echo of the early PCs (the ancient *kilobyte* equalled 1,024 *bits* of data).

There is no central controller in a starship's computer; each of the ten levels within the core work together to satisfy the computing needs of the entire ship. This *parallel processing* is common on all general-purpose computers in use within the Federation. Although familiar today, the technique of parallel processing dates back to the late twentieth century on Earth; ironically, most personal computers of that era did not employ it. Instead they utilized a form of logical task division called *vector processing*. This more primitive system allowed special chips called *math co-processors* to assume some of the arithmetic functions, while the *CPU (central processing unit)* carried out other tasks simultaneously. The main computering process of a twentieth-century PC could be divided into only two *paths*—the CPU path and the MPU (math processor unit) path. Though ingenious, this early solution was long obsolete by the time of the first interstellar flights.

A series of subprocessor nodes located throughout a *Galaxy* class starship perform the first layer of processing. In the event of complete core failure, these subprocessors can perform needed computer operations, although at a greatly reduced speed. Under normal conditions, minor processes are performed by these subprocessors, which pass additional processing requests to the central core through the optical data network (ODN). In order for processes to be divided and distributed, the subprocessor nodes divide logical processes into their smallest components, and assign each process a unique core address which in turn distributes simultaneous computer requests among the core clusters. This logical division of tasks takes place within a theoretical space called a *hypercube*. (This term dates back to studies first conducted at the Massachusetts Institute of Technology, the forerunner of Earth's Global Intelligence Consortium.)

The techniques for subdividing logical processes originated (logically enough) on Vulcan. The Surakian philosophy of isological primes allows Vulcans to calculate analyses without the aid of computers. This deductive technique was translated into a computer algorithm around Stardate 959.1. That breakthrough was directly responsible for the design of all Vulcan and (and later, all computers used within the Federation), including those currently installed aboard *Galaxy* class starships.

# Inside the System Unit of a Twentieth-Century PC

**CPU**—As computers grew in complexity and shrank in size, specialized components called *microprocessors* were developed. The microprocessor (also called the *CPU* or *central processing unit*) became the personal computer's equivalent of a "brain." Although simple by our present-day standards, the CPU was a hardworking brain. When an application (program) was started by the user, the CPU would load the first group of program instructions and data into memory (see RAM later in this section). The CPU then processed the first program instruction, moving onto the next instruction, until the job was completed. (An *instruction* was a program statement that the CPU could understand and execute, such as an instruction to read a piece of data or add two numbers together.) A program instruction often required the CPU to obtain data from memory and process it, after which, that data was placed back in memory where the program could examine the results. In addition, the CPU might pass these program instructions on to other computer components (such as the memory, video, or disk drive controllers)—these components would then fill the request, leaving the CPU free to process the next instruction. You will learn more about the method in which the CPU processed information later in this chapter.

RAM or *random access memory* contained the data that the PC was currently processing. In RAM, data was stored as the presence or absence of an electronic charge within a series of microchips called RAM or memory chips. RAM was electronic; any data placed there while the PC was in operation was subsequently erased if an energy fluctuation resulted in a temporary power loss (or if the user shut off the PC deliberately). Later in this chapter, you will learn how these memory chips actually stored this pattern of electrical charges.

The core memory of *Galaxy* class starships consists of 2,048 modules of 144 isolinear chips each. Each module can store approximately 630,000 kiloquads of information. An isolinear chip works by storing its data optically. Although optical storage technology replaced RAM centuries ago, the ancient secret of RAM storage (electronically-charged particles within a silicon-based microchip) is still rewarding to study. Later in this chapter, you will learn more about it.

*A close study of these early computers reveals just how consistently they imitated certain human neurological processes, even then. The CPU was analogous to the decision-making part of the cerebrum. RAM behaved like short-term memory; the hard disk served as the PC's long-term memory. The monitor was the PC's voice—its means of communication. The bus functioned like a central nervous system—conveying "nerve impulses" of data between the PC's "cerebrum" and its various components.*

**—Dr. Beverly Crusher, Chief Medical Officer, U.S.S. Enterprise**

# System Unit

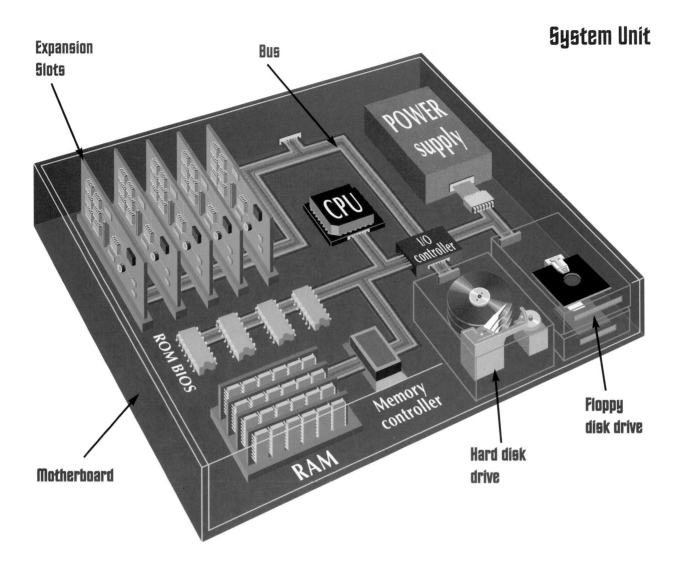

**Expansion Slots**

**Bus**

POWER supply

CPU

I/O controller

ROM BIOS

Memory controller

**Motherboard**

RAM

**Hard disk drive**

**Floppy disk drive**

**ROM** or *read only memory* was contained on several microchips similar in size and shape to a RAM chip, but in which the information had been permanently etched. The instructions that the PC needed to carry out its basic functions were stored in ROM. These basic instructions included moving data in and out of RAM for processing, storing data permanently on magnetic media, displaying information on a screen, and interpreting commands typed on a keyboard. ROM also performed a series of tests when the PC was turned on, to determine whether the PC was functioning properly.

**ROM BIOS**—The most important of the ROM instructions were collectively called BIOS, or *basic input-output system.* Anytime input or output to and from the PC was needed, ROM BIOS controlled it. ROM BIOS helped the central processor (CPU) manipulate data between RAM and the input/output devices such as the keyboard, monitor, printer, modem, and disk drives.

*Controllers were single purpose processors for high-traffic components such as memory, disk drives, and the monitor.*

**Motherboard**—The circuit board into which all computer components were connected was called the **motherboard**, or sometimes the *system board.* ROM, RAM, the CPU, and special *controllers* were connected to the motherboard through sockets from which they could be removed for repair.

> *Another important function of ROM was to boot (initiate) the CPU when the PC was first "powered on" (put in operation). I cannot explain the use of the word "boot" because there is no existing evidence that explains the method in which the human foot was involved in this power-on process.*
>
> **—Lt. Commander Data**

*A sound board was a digital-to-analog converter—capable of converting digitally recorded sound into audio output.*

**Expansion slots**—General-purpose sockets called *expansion slots* were built into the motherboard to accommodate add-on devices. Users inserted *expansion boards,* aptly named because they *expanded* the normal function of the computer, into these expansion slots. For example, most computers were not capable of more than a rudimentary sound unless a *sound card* was added through one of these expansion slots. (You will learn more about how the PC manufactured sound in Chapter 4.)

**Bus**—The bus was a series of interconnecting electrical leads which carried signals from one computer component to another. The bus was the component through which the various parts of the PC (the CPU, RAM, the disk drives, monitor, printer) communicated. Data travelled along the bus, accompanied by the address to which the data was moving. The internal clock signal which kept all the PC components in synch also traveled along the bus. For example, when data was transferred from permanent storage to memory (RAM), it traveled along the bus. When signals were sent to the printer or the monitor—requiring that the contents of memory be printed or displayed—these signals also traveled along the bus. In addition, the expansion slots were connected to the bus, allowing them to communicate with the CPU.

**Hard disk drive**—A permanent storage area for data (such as letters, reports, and graphics), in addition to the *programs* used to create the data. Inside the hard disk drive were individual platters (disks) covered on both sides with a special magnetic material. By rearranging metallic particles within the magnetic material, data could be stored on both sides of the platters.

**Floppy disk drive**—Similar to the PC's hard drive, a floppy disk drive stored data on magnetic material. There was one important difference between a floppy disk drive and a hard drive—the magnetic material used in a floppy disk drive was encased in a plastic container which could be removed from the drive, rendering the data stored on the diskette transportable from one PC to another. These transportable storage units were called *diskettes*; earlier versions were called floppy disks because of the flexible material of which they were made. Another major difference between a hard disk and a diskette, however, was storage capacity: a typical diskette stored roughly 1/200th as much data as the average hard disk.

**Power supply**—Each PC had a *power supply*—a rugged device that provided power to the PC's internal components. In addition, the power supply converted the AC (alternating current) of the period to DC (direct current). The conversion was necessary because the PC used direct current and household power was alternating current. Because the logic of the PC was formed of switching electrical pulses, the components—especially the CPU and the RAM chips—got very hot, so the power supply also contained a fan which cooled the internal components.

Unlike the computers on a starship, which must always be active, PCs of the twentieth century were often shut down at the end of the day. Many people believed (and rightly) that this practice protected their vulnerable computers from power surges and overheating. "Powering down" a PC posed no particular problems, since typically it would be used by a single person for intermittent personal tasks, and not for ongoing tasks such as controlling the environment or navigating a ship.

In contrast, the processing cores on a starship are not shut down unless they are being upgraded, or unless they experience a power failure. In such a case, one of the two redundant processing cores performs the processing for the disabled core.

*Our ship's computers were once upgraded by a race of beings that conversed entirely in binary code. It would be interesting to determine whether the thought processes of Bynar mirror the operation of the ancient CPU—which also conveyed information entirely in binary code.*

—**Lt. Commander Deanna Troi,
Counselor, U.S.S. Enterprise**

# A Closer Look at the CPU or Microprocessor

The microprocessor (CPU) processed the PC's data and instructions. By the close of the twentieth century, the most popular CPUs were the 486 (the informal name for the Intel 486 chip) and the Pentium (essentially, the Intel 586, though it was never actually sold under that name). The CPU was an integrated circuit made up of millions of *transistors* (miniaturized ON/OFF switches). The Pentium contained over 3.1 million of these transistors.

The 486 and the Pentium CPUs differed slightly in the way they processed data, but most of the processes involved were the same. Since the Pentium was the most advanced microprocessor of its time, we will take a closer look at it.

1. The Bus Interface Unit retrieved information from RAM (memory), and placed it in either the *Data Cache (if it was data) or the Code Cache* (if it was a program instruction). These caches were temporary storage areas within the CPU where information awaited processing.

2. The code in the Code Cache was then analyzed by the Branch Predictor to determine the best way for the CPU to process it. The Pentium CPU had two internal *instruction pipelines* through which it could process two *different* instructions simultaneously, and the Branch Predictor determined which of these two pipelines to use. (The "pipe" metaphor was inspired by actual Earth waterworks, but in this case the flow of data, not water, was being directed.)

3. Once the proper instruction path was determined, the code moved from the Code Cache to the Prefetch Buffer, where it was held until the Instruction Decode Unit prepared the instruction for execution.

4. Non-integer math (such as the plotting of a particular point on the screen) was passed on to the Floating Point Unit. This unit processed it and placed the result in the Data Cache.

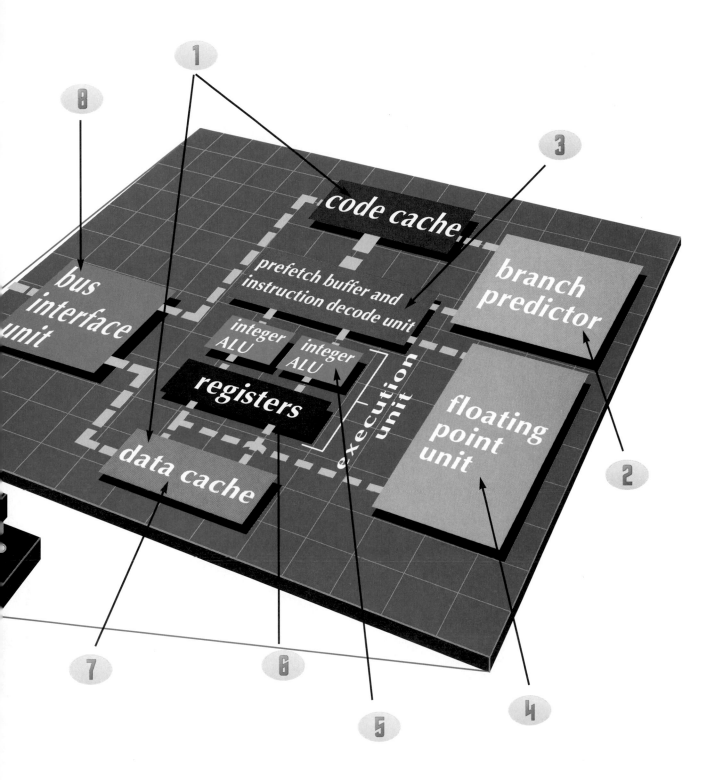

1

8

3

code cache

prefetch buffer and
instruction decode unit

branch
predictor

bus
interface
unit

integer
ALU

integer
ALU

execution unit

registers

floating
point
unit

2

data cache

7

6

5

4

*These two pipelines, together with their registers (temporary storage areas) were collectively called the Execution Unit.*

5. The Instruction Decode Unit placed the remaining program instructions one by one, onto the proper instruction pipeline. Each pipeline had its own Arithmetic Logic Unit (ALU)—a high-speed circuit within the CPU which performed the actual calculations and comparisons.

6. Meanwhile, any data that the ALUs might need in order to perform a particular calculation was moved from the Data Cache to one of the registers.

7. The ALUs performed their calculations and placed the results in the Data Cache.

8. The Bus Interface Unit sent the resulting data through the bus, on its way to storage in RAM. All of this took approximately 8 billionths of a second per instruction.

The 486 belonged to a family of processors manufactured by a company called Intel (which you might recognize as the ancestor of the Intel-Flynn Optichip Company today). Intel's earliest (and slowest) CPUs were labeled with numbers such as 8088 and 8086. Later improved models (slightly faster) bore more impressive numbers—80286, 386, and 486—the "80" designation was removed early on.

Considered fast for its time, the 486 processed about 54 **million instructions per second** (MIPS). The 586 (Pentium) processed more than twice that amount: 112 million instructions per second. Released near the end of the twentieth century, the Pentium might not compare well to its faster descendants in starship computers (which process instructions at near lightspeed), but it was undeniably an impressive achievement.

*The Bynars are the only Federation race who converse in binary code.*

# The PC's Bus

The personal computer's **bus** carried signals along a complex route from one computer component to another. (Note that although the bus itself looked physically like an indecipherable mess of etched circuits on the motherboard, it is displayed in this figure as a simple path leading from component to component.) The CPU used the bus as its communications link with RAM, the disk drive controllers, and the PC's other components. The bus connected to the CPU through its Bus Interface Unit (see the previous section for a detailed description of the internal workings of the CPU). It was the function of the Bus Interface Unit to retrieve data for the CPU, and to place it back in RAM after the CPU was finished processing it. In addition, the Bus Interface Unit placed other signals (not just data) on the bus. The signals on the bus were composed of three separate components —*data*, *address* (the address to which data was to be read or written), and *control* (signals indicating whether data was moving to or from the CPU). Curiously enough, even though the PC had only one bus, each of the seperate functions of that bus (data, address, and control) were known as buses in and of themselves.

The amount of data the Bus Interface Unit could retrieve at one time was determined by the *data width* of the CPU. The Pentium had the largest data width of its day: a full 64 *bits* (or eight *bytes*). Its immediate predecessors, the 486 and 386 CPUs, had only a 32-bit data width (four bytes).

Within the *U.S.S. Enterprise's* computer core, data travels at faster-than-light speeds. This is possible through the employment of a subspace field called a *hypercube field* maintained around the core elements. Information is then sent (or *bussed*, to use a twentieth-century term) through the ship's optical data network (ODN) until it reaches a display panel.

The amount of data that could be placed on the PC's *data* bus varied according to the type of microprocessor employed. (The Pentium had a 64-bit data bus, which eclipsed the 32-bit bus of the 386 and 486 CPUs.) A byte, which was the amount of space required to store a single character, was comprised of eight bits. The Pentium data bus was capable of moving 64-bits of data at one time, or 8 bytes (characters). A 32-bit bus was capable of moving 4 bytes (characters) at one time. The size of a CPU's *address bus* limited the amount of RAM the CPU could access. Each of the three most popular CPUs of the twentieth century (386, 486, and Pentium) used a 32-bit address bus enabling them to access 232 addresses, or 4 gigabytes of RAM (memory). The *control bus* carried various types of electrical signals. One such signal indicated whether data was being sent *to* or *from* the CPU. Another signal (the clock signal) helped to synchronize all operations within the computer.

*Expansion slots* were general-purpose connections that allowed the PC to be easily upgraded or expanded. The expansion slots were connected to the bus. There were several varieties of expansion slots, each capable of transferring only a specific amount of data to the bus during a single clock cycle. There were four types of expansion buses used in PCs in the late 1900s: 8-bit, ISA, EISA, and Micro Channel, and they transferred anywhere from 8 to 32 bits of data at a time.

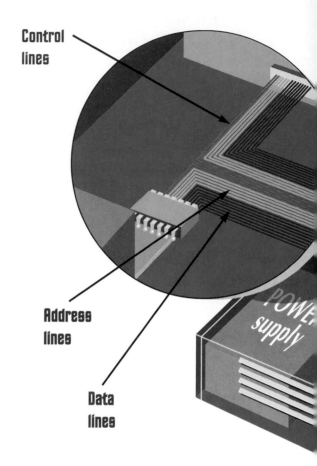

**Control lines**

**Address lines**

**Data lines**

Micro Channel Architecture (MCA) was a standard for expansion buses that was developed by IBM (International Business Machines). IBM was a leader in the computing industry throughout the twentieth and twenty-first centuries, setting industry standards that the numerous other PC manufacturers followed. When IBM introduced its PC in 1981, it was an instant success—the design of the IBM PC became the model upon which an industry was built. Although Micro Channel Architecture was not incorporated in a majority of PCs other than IBM, it focused interest on 32-bit expansion buses which led to the standards set by the EISA bus.

Data was transferred between the CPU and an expansion slot at a rate which equalled the bit width of the slot, not the data width of the CPU. For example, if a PC was equipped with a Pentium CPU and an ISA expansion slot, data was transferred 16 bits at a time (the bit width of the ISA slot). (This ridiculous situation would make such a PC much less efficient, since the Pentium CPU was capable of sending and receiving data 64 bits at a time).

In addition, data transfers from the CPU to any I/O port (such as the disk drives, the printer, or the monitor) was often matched to the bit transfer rate of the expansion slots— so if a PC had ISA expansion slots, I/O transfers occurred at a rate of 16 bits at a time. For relatively slow-working devices such as disk drives and printers, this was not really a problem. But for monitors that could accept data at a faster rate, this was a serious limitation.

## Components of the Bus

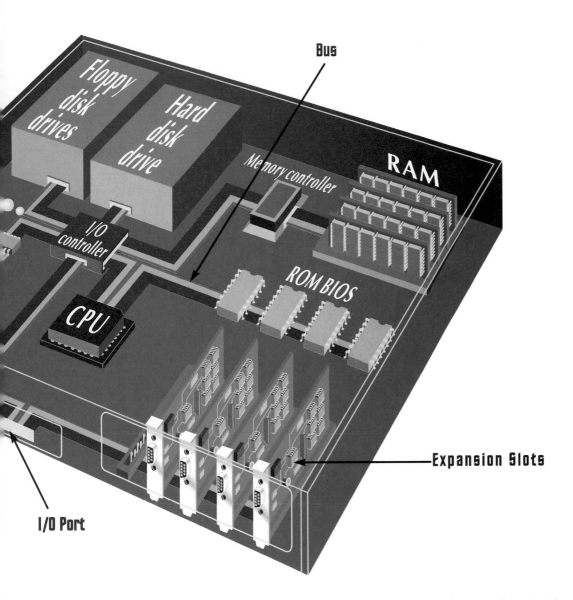

Bus

Floppy disk drives

Hard disk drive

Memory controller

RAM

I/O controller

ROM BIOS

CPU

Expansion Slots

I/O Port

Through the use of a *local bus* which connected the CPU directly to a particular peripheral, data transfer rates were improved. If such a bus was used to connect the video controller directly to the CPU, data could travel over the local bus at the CPU's own speed (60 Mhz or faster) and data width (usually 32 to 64 bits). This meant the data path to the monitor was now clear and fast, no longer bound by the same slow speed used for every I/O device.

# A Closer Look at RAM

*The isolinear chips used in computers throughout the Federation are similar to form and function of twentieth-century RAM microchips. However, RAM chips were used exclusively for the temporary storage of data—unlike isolinear chips, which are used for both temporary and permanent storage of data.*

—**Lt. Commander Data, Operations Manager, U.S.S. Enterprise**

**RAM** (or *random access memory*) was the PC's "working area;" programs and data had to be "loaded" into RAM before they could be processed by the CPU, and work could be done. A RAM chip was a collection of transistors (switches which could be turned ON or OFF), controlling the flow of electrici-ty to individual capacitors. When electricity was allowed to flow through the transistor, the capacitors stored the electrical charge so it could be read later. If a capacitor registered a charge, it was thought to represent a 1, with no charge, the capacitor represented a 0. Every letter, every number within the PC, was expressed as a series of 1's and 0's. For example, the letter **d** was stored as **01100100**.

RAM was organized into *bytes*, comprised of eight *bits* each; a bit was represented as a single 1 or 0. Therefore, to store the letter **d** (01100100) in RAM required one byte (eight bits) of memory. To organize all these bytes within RAM, each byte of memory was given a specific address number, starting with 0. When the CPU needed to read what was stored in a particular byte in RAM, it used this address.

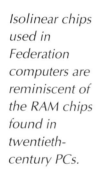

*Isolinear chips used in Federation computers are reminiscent of the RAM chips found in twentieth-century PCs.*

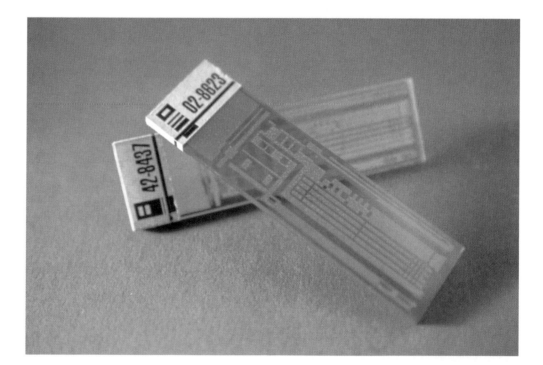

When the CPU needed to access something in RAM, it placed its memory address on the *address bus*. The memory address traveled down the address bus to the memory controller. In addition, the CPU placed a control signal on the bus, notifying the memory controller that an address was ready to be read. The memory controller then determined which row of memory chips contained the memory address.

Next, the memory controller sent an electrical charge down the address line, preparing each chip in that row to receive data. With the address line holding each chip "open," a second electrical charge was sent down the data line, turning "on" a single transistor within the appropriate chips. This formed the pattern for a single byte of data. For the letter **d**, the pattern **01100100** was sent.

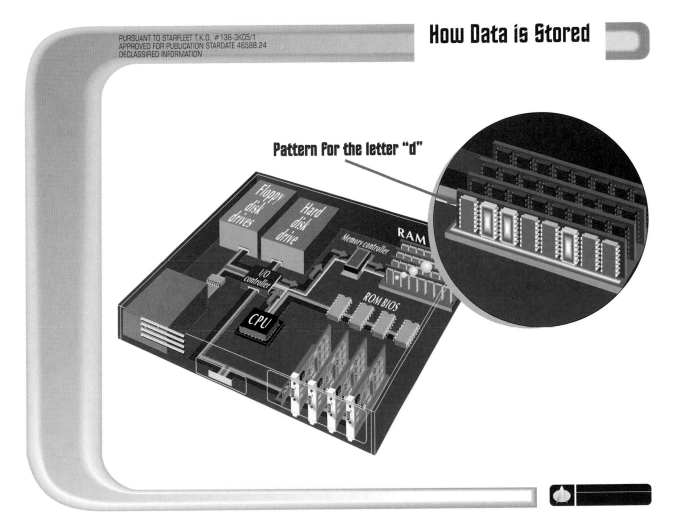

## How Data is Stored

PURSUANT TO STARFLEET T.K.O. #136-3K05/1
APPROVED FOR PUBLICATION STARDATE 46588.24
DECLASSIFIED INFORMATION

Pattern for the letter "d"

Floppy disk drives

Hard disk drive

Memory controller

RAM

I/O controller

ROM BIOS

CPU

The time it took to read or write a byte of memory depended on the type of microprocessor in the PC and the size of its data bus. The Pentium accessed 8 bytes (64 bits) of data within a single tick of its internal clock. By contrast, the 386 CPU took two clock cycles to access a mere two bytes (16 bits) of data in RAM.

The 386, 486, and Pentium microprocessors each had a 32-bit address bus, which meant that they were capable of generating unique addresses for up to 4096 megabytes of RAM. This did not mean, however, that PCs actually *did* access this much RAM; they were restricted by the limitations of their *operating systems*. The Microsoft Disk Operating System (**MS-DOS**) was the most popular operating system at the time, but even so, MS-DOS was capable of directly addressing only 1 megabyte of memory. Despite such limits, special software was used to help the CPU access the additional memory over 1 MB—for more information, refer to chapter 9.

Despite such limitations, MS-DOS was to have a distinguished history. It was used in PCs from 1978 until circa 1995 (when its dominance was usurped by more powerful operating systems), but it did not disappear entirely. It was still in use late into the twenty-second century: several penal colonies used a form of MS-DOS as an inexpensive method for controlling their lighting systems.

A single RAM chip contained several transistors, making it capable of storing not a single bit, but several. Average chip capacity was anywhere from 256 kilobytes to 16 megabytes per chip. (A kilobyte was equal to 1024 bytes, a megabyte was equal to 1024 kilobytes.)

Although the physical arrangement of RAM chips within a PC varied, logically, nine RAM chips comprised a single row of memory. When a byte of data was written to RAM, eight of these chips performed the function of storing a single bit of that data; eight bits equaled a byte, which was the smallest amount of data typically stored in memory. The ninth chip was a *parity* chip—an "error-control chip" which was used to verify the data stored in the other eight chips.

*If you took a look at the processing cores in a Galaxy class starship, you might notice they bear a certain resemblance to the system units of twentieth-century PCs. This isn't really that unusual; even modern computer architecture incorporates the best ideas of many different worlds. Some of these include the classical computer designs first discussed on Earth in the twentieth century. In our processing cores, there is an area for temporary storage similar to the early RAM, and an area where data is stored permanently (similar to a PC's hard disk). LCARS, which controls the processing of data in our systems, is really just an advanced replacement for the combination of hardware (CPU, ROM) and software that processed data in the early PCs.*

—*Lt. Commander Geordi La Forge, Chief of Engineering, U.S.S. Enterprise*

# Chapter Three

# A Closer Look at the Microchip

In the Smithsonian Museum of Computer History, there exist many functional twentieth-century computer components. For me, the most fascinating of these is an intact, working microchip. Its composition, and its storage process are clear forerunners of later data storage techniques—even the isolinear chip itself, invented in the late twenty-third century, incorporates the design of these early microchips in its basic structure.

Indeed, even the origin of term "microchip" is interesting, as it tells us something of its manufacturers and their techniques. A microchip was actually a small piece (a chip) of a larger wafer of processed silicon—the large wafer was formed using the process described here, and then cut into tiny microchips. Careful analysis of surviving microchips has given us a remarkably detailed picture of the process involved in their manufacture. I think you will agree that the microchip was elegant in its simple technology.

—Captain Jean-Luc Picard, U.S.S. Enterprise

The microchip was a crucial step forward for the twentieth-century PC. With the invention of the microchip, computers could be made smaller, faster, and more powerful for less money (credits). The microchip turned PCs into affordable alternatives to the time-honored (but slower) methods of data collection and organization—many of which were still done by hand.

The discovery of *semiconductors* made the microchip possible. Formed of elements such as silicon and germanium, a semiconductor was a unique electronic component: one which did not conduct electricity, and yet did not quite prevent electricity from moving through it. When a small charge of electricity was applied to a semiconductor, it changed from a non-conductor to a conductor of electricity. Computer design engineers now had a *controllable* conductor of electricity that could be miniaturized, enabling relatively small (desktop) personal computers to be manufactured.

As you learned in the last chapter, RAM (and many other PC components, including the CPU) was really just a set of complex ON/OFF switches. The data stored in a PC was binary, meaning that it had only two states: 0 and 1. These two states could be represented electronically with tiny ON/OFF switches. Earlier in the twentieth century, computers were constructed with vacuum tubes (devices which controlled the flow of electricity in a vacuum)—but these computers were entirely too large to fit on a desktop (most of them occupied entire rooms). So it wasn't until the semiconductor was invented that a miniaturized "switch" existed, enabling in turn, the miniaturization of the computer itself.

But a PC was more than just a series of ON/OFF switches—most PC components were a combination of several electrical devices: transistors, capacitors, and resistors. Using semiconductors, a single chip of silicon was formed into a complex, *integrated circuit*—a miniaturized, self-contained collection of electronic components. In a microchip, *transistors* served as ON/OFF switches (creating the 1s and 0s of a bit). *Capacitors* held that charge (allowing a bit to keep its value of 0 or 1). *Resistors* controlled electricity and forced it to flow in one direction creating logic within the PC—a program could instruct the CPU to do one thing if something was true, and another thing if it were not. The resistor forced electricity to flow in a single direction based on the charge of neighboring components, and that direction was then interpreted by the CPU as "Yes" or "No." Such sophistication on a tiny scale made the microchip a giant leap in technology, beyond the purely mechanical storage and logic devices of early computers. This chapter explores the ancient secret of a microchip's manufacture, and how it was used by the PC to store information.

# How a Microchip Was Built

The manufacturing of a microchip was a painstaking process, and a brilliant use of known physics and chemistry. In truth, it is far more accurate to say that a microchip was "grown" rather than built. A microchip was created by growing micro-thin layers of silicon; impurities were then added deliberately, in a process called *doping*. The doping resulted in silicon material that was either full of electrons (therefore, registering a charge of electricity) or deficient in electrons (therefore, registering no charge). The electrically charged silicon was called n-doped; the silicon with no charge was p-doped.

The specific type of impurity during the doping process was what caused the silicon crystals to conduct electricity different ways. Negative doping produced *n-doped* silicon, which conducted electricity through the free movement of electrons which have a negative charge. Positive doping produced *p-doped* silicon, which permitted conduction by allowing electron *sites* to drift (holes in the crystal silicon lattice of the microchip, where passing electrons could be held temporarily).

A microchip was comprised of these tiny wells of n-doped and p-doped silicon—these wells formed the tiny circuitry needed to create all the components of an integrated circuit: transistors, capacitors, and resistors. To manufacture a microchip, a technician inserted a p-doped silicon wafer into a chamber where heat was applied. He or she then pumped silicon chloride gas with a negative impurity (phosphorus) into the chamber. As a result, negative crystals grew on the surface of the wafer. The result was a silicon wafer with a p-doped substrate (under-surface), covered with a thin layer of negatively-charged (n-doped) silicon.

*The growth of crystals from a vapor was called epitaxial growth. This method was the preferred twentieth-century technique for forming silicon layers.*

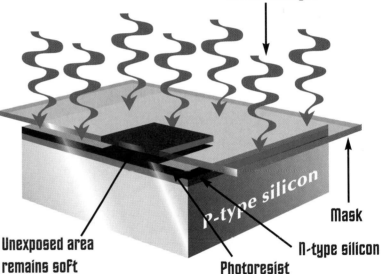

**Ultraviolet light**

**Mask**

**N-type silicon**

**Photoresist**

**Unexposed area remains soft**

p-type silicon

Once the n-doped (N-type) surface was in place, a layer of light-sensitive film called *photoresist* was applied to the wafer. A design was transferred onto this surface by selectively exposing sections of the photoresist to ultraviolet light. Using a mask which blocked some of the ultraviolet light, selected regions were prevented from being exposed. These protected regions remained soft; only the exposed areas of the photoresist hardened.

The soft (unexposed) areas of the photoresist were then dissolved or etched away, forming tiny windows in the silicon. Next, the wafer was exposed to an ion beam. Electrons from the beam entered the wafer's exposed regions.

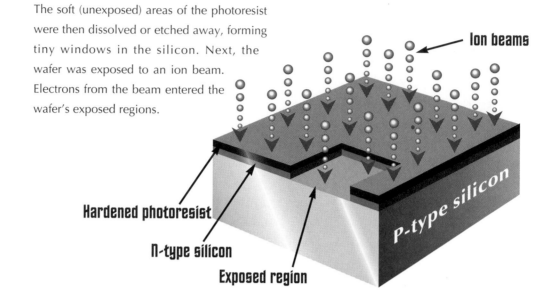

**Ion beams**

**Hardened photoresist**

**N-type silicon**

**Exposed region**

**p-type silicon**

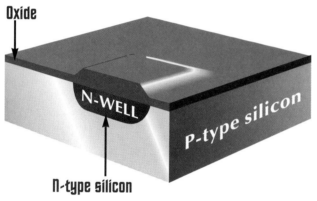

**Oxide**

**N-WELL**

**p-type silicon**

**N-type silicon**

When heated, the ion-exposed regions grew, creating *n-wells*. A layer of oxide was applied, sealing the openings. This entire cycle was repeated, growing and etching layer after layer of silicon, until the desired n-type and p-type regions were created. (To grow p-type regions, selected areas were exposed to a different kind of beam.)

Finally, a last set of windows was cut into the surface of the silicon, and a layer of gold or aluminum was deposited. Metal wires would later be attached to these leads, connecting the integrated circuit with the outside world of the computer.

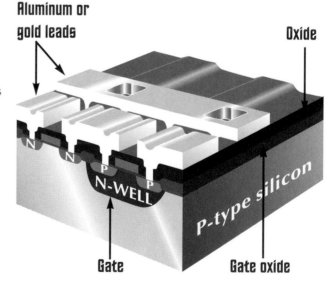

**Aluminum or gold leads**

**Oxide**

**N-WELL**

**p-type silicon**

**Gate**

**Gate oxide**

# How a Microchip Stored Information

Data within a personal computer was stored as a series of 1s and 0s (more accurately, the presence or absence of electrical charges). The transistor was the most crucial part of the microchip, because it could switch the value of a *binary digit* (*bit*). A binary digit existed in one of two states: "on" or "off," which was thought of in numerical terms as being equal to 1 or 0. A combination of 8 bits formed a single *byte*—each unique pattern of 8 bits represented different letters, decimal numbers, and other symbols within the electronic world of the PC.

In addition to representing data through the presence or absence of an electrical charge, a bit was used to control the CPU's *logic gates*—its primary decision-making process. To determine which action to take in a particular instance, the CPU compared two incoming bits within its logic gates. Depending on the value of each comparison bit and the type of comparison taking place, a resulting bit was created (again, 1 or 0). The resulting bit (the 1 or the 0) caused the CPU to take one of two actions. The electrical logic of the CPU's logic gates mimicked mathematical logic—specifically, a form of mathematical logic developed on Earth by the mathematician George Boole in the calendar year 1856. It is for Boole that *Boolean* logic gates were named.

*The idea that a machine could make "guesses" was not really explored until late in the twentieth century. You'll read about these experiments in "artificial intelligence" and "fuzzy logic" later in this course. But even though the incredible advances of Dr. Noonian Soong have resulted in a credible poker player in Data, a machine can only go so far—I mean, I have yet to find one that can beat me at poker.*

**—Commander William T. Riker,**
**Executive Officer, U.S.S. Enterprise**

*"I have yet to find a computer that can beat me at poker."*
**—Commander Riker, U.S.S. Enterprise**

The early PCs weren't designed to mimic the human thought-process—and that was just as well, because it would have been beyond the capabilities of the time. Instead, they were general-purpose machines, designed to perform whatever task they were given. If you could break the task down into small enough steps, you could get your PC to perform it.

The logical 1s and 0s which comprised a PC's data and logic patterns were simply the presence or absence of electrical charges. Deep within the complex circuitry of each microchip, transistors formed the binary-switching control, switching 1s to 0s and back again. Every transistor had n-doped or p-doped regions, and each of those regions acted as an *emitter*, a *base*, or a *collector* for the transistor. When an electrical charge was applied to base area, electrons would flow from the emitter (also called the source) through the base to the collector (also called the drain). The following section describes how a logical 0 was changed to a logical 1 within a transistor.

There were many different types of Boolean comparisons which the CPU could perform. For example, the CPU could be instructed to compare the two bits to see if they were both equal to 1, and render the result of 1 only if they were both 1, and a 0 in all other cases. Variations of this simple comparison could create different results—for example, the CPU could be told to render a 1 if either one of the bits were equal to 1, and to render a 0 only if they were both equal to 0.

## How a Transistor Works

In their natural state, electrons from the *source* diffused into the surrounding *base* of the transistor. Once the electrons had built up to a certain level in the base, they would remain motionless. At this stage, the drain did not have enough electrons to register a charge, so the transistor was set to "0."

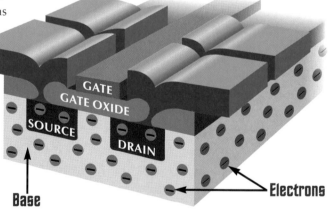

GATE
GATE OXIDE
SOURCE
DRAIN
Base
Electrons

When it was necessary to change the bit to 1, a small electrical charge was applied to the gate. The gate was the part of the transistor that triggered the change in the transistor's electrical charge; the gate was also known as a "voltage-actuated control terminal." This charge of electricity traveled downward through the gate oxide, into the part of the base nearest the gate.

**Electrical charge**

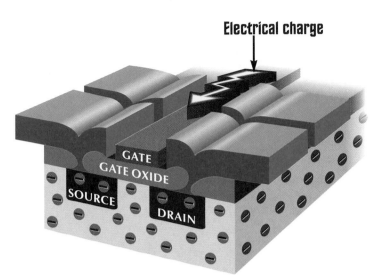

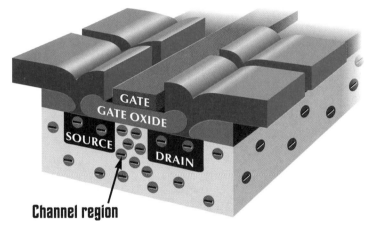

**Channel region**

Negatively-charged electrons in the base traveled upward to the positively-charged gate. They concentrated in a region called the *channel.*

As the channel was filled with a negative charge, electrons flowed from the *source* (emitter) to the *drain* (collector). This completed the circuit. The transistor was "on," that is, set to **1**.

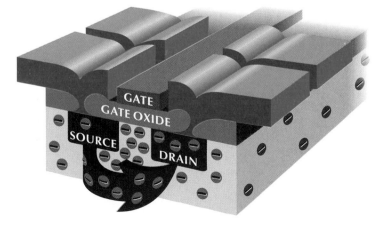

When the electrical charge was removed, the electrons once again diffused, and eventually became inert. Since the flow of electrons was halted, the circuit was broken. This meant the transistor was turned "off," or set to **0**.

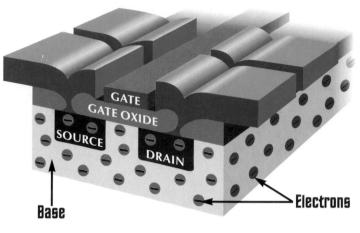

As you might recall from your Starfleet Academy courses on logic, the base component of all logic is the binary state (true/false, yes/no, on/off). Although on Earth it was George Boole who first conceived the notion of representing logic through mathematical formulas, it was actually the Austrian John von Neumann who first realized that a binary state could be represented by a transistor. He therefore concluded that all logical processes could be represented and executed electronically, using transistor components. Although Von Neumann did not build Earth's first electronic computers himself, those who did called their creations "von Neumann machines" in his honor, a tribute often obscured by subsequent history.

*The invention of the isolinear chip created a milestone in computing history, similar in impact to the invention of the microchip in the twentieth century. Both chips vastly improved the capabilities of contemporary computers by increasing storage capabilities while improving the speed of data retrieval. The impact of such innovations on the history of computing cannot be overstated.*

—Elizabeth Megry, Instructor (Computer Theories),
Starfleet Academy

# Chapter Four

# Input Devices

Computer games were so popular on twentieth-century Earth that some humans of that era joked about being "addicted" to them. However, addiction to such games became a serious reality for the crew of the Enterprise when I received a recreational device from a woman I met on shore leave on the planet Risa. Etana was later revealed to be a military operative of the Ktarans—the headset she gave me was not a game at all, but a device that employed neural-optical conditioning techniques to ultimately take control of its user. The headset stimulated certain portions of the brain, and caused the user to see floating disks that had to be maneuvered into tubes—after which the user would be "reward-ed" with a tremendous feeling of pleasure. The reward was highly addictive, and if it were not for the intervention of Lieutenant Commander Data, visiting Starfleet Cadet Wesley Crusher, and Mission Specialist Robin Lefler, the Ktaran plot to control Starfleet might have been successful. In the future, if I want to program some new entertainment, I'll stick to more conventional input devices—such as voice recognizers and sensor panels.

—Commander William T. Riker, Executive Officer,
U.S.S. Enterprise

# The Keyboard

*It's interesting to me that the keyboard predominated as the main method of input, despite its potential as a health hazard. The repeated motion of pressing the keys—thousands upon thousands of times a day—led to a debilitating condition of the hand called "Carpal Tunnel Syndrome." A compression of the main nerve to the hand caused this painful condition. Standard keyboards of the twentieth century forced the wrists into an unnatural position (pointed slightly outwards), aggravating the onset of the condition.*

*Several alternative keyboard designs were invented to help prevent this terrible condition, including split keyboards, and keyboards that were operated with one hand. But it was considered a practical necessity to continue producing one standard type of keyboard. This prevented any real acceptance of a design change. The most common solution was to place a padded device called a "wrist rest" in front of the keyboard, which raised the wrists to a more comfortable typing position. It was not until voice recognition was fully developed that the keyboard began to lose its popularity, and fewer users had to risk Carpal Tunnel Syndrome.*

**—Dr. Beverly Crusher, Chief Medical Officer, U.S.S. Enterprise**

The PCs of the twentieth century provided many ways for the user to issue commands and to input data. Some of the devices employed for inputting commands were tactile (keyboard or touch screens), some were motion-sensitive (mouse or graphic tablets), some were light-sensitive (light pens and scanners), while others were sound-sensitive (microphones). The most widely used of all these devices was the keyboard.

The predominance of the keyboard as a method of PC input is more easily understood when you consider it in within the context of the technology available at the time. Toward the end of the twentieth century, voice-recognition devices were just beginning to be developed so they were not in wide-spread use. Mouse-driven graphical interfaces such as Windows were just beginning to find widespread acceptance, while graphic tablets, light pens, and scanners were devices used mostly by specialized industries. The basic keyboard design was familiar to the majority of PC users because it had been adapted from earlier mechanical writing machines called typewriters. Its familiar method of operation was an advantage, despite its limitations as an input device.

Although several versions of the PC keyboard existed, the most common version was the *Enhanced* keyboard (also called the *101* keyboard for its number of keys). It was introduced with the IBM AT in 1984. Other keyboard manufacturers made slight changes (such as moving the arrow keys, or adding a second row of function keys), but the basic function of all PC keyboards remained the same. In chapter 1, you learned that when a key was pressed, a change occurred in the electrical current associated with that key. This change was significant enough so that the keyboard CPU could identify which key had been pressed. There were only two methods employed to cause this change in electrical current, so all keyboards fell into two categories: *mechanical* (or *capacitive*) keyboards—which often accompanied each keypress with a soft audible click—and *membrane* (or *hard contact*) keyboards, which were less durable than their mechanical cousins (and virtually silent).

A mechanical (capacitive) keyboard worked by spreading apart two electrical contacts, causing a change (a lowering) in the electrical current whenever a key was pressed.

A membrane (hard-contact) keyboard also worked by changing the flow of electric current. However, instead of breaking the connection (like a mechanical keyboard), pressing a key on a membrane keyboard allowed two membranes to touch, which *completed* the electrical connection.

## Mechanical Keyboard

## Membrane Keyboard

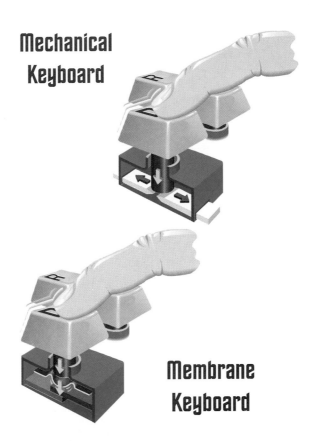

The PADD (personal access display device) features an easy-to-use keypad.

# The Mouse

A *mouse* was a palm-sized device used for visually selecting commands by manipulating an on-screen pointer. As the mouse was rolled on a flat surface in one direction or the other, the pointer moved correspondingly across the screen. The first mouse was invented on Earth in 1963 by Doug Englebart at the Stanford Research Institute. The mouse was not invented for use with PCs (they did not exist yet), but as a way to eliminate the need to design unique control panels for each program on a mainframe computer.

A mouse was either *mechanical* or *optical*. A mechanical mouse typically contained a ball of rubber or some other urethane substance which was partially exposed on its underside. The movement of a mechanical mouse was gauged by the movement of this ball. An optical mouse emitted a light, and when rolled over a special pad, photo detectors inside the optical mouse sensed the light's moving reflection. In this section, you will learn the details of how a mechanical mouse worked. An optical mouse worked similarly to a trackball, which is covered in the next section.

Desktop terminals, such as those often used in starship conference rooms, provide full computer access in a minimum of space. The control panel of desktop terminals contains a small number of keypads for controlling the display of data. In addition, a device which works in a manner similar to a twentieth century mouse is located in the center of the keypad area.

*With its small number of keypads and its built-in "mouse," a desktop terminal provides a simple means of accessing data.*

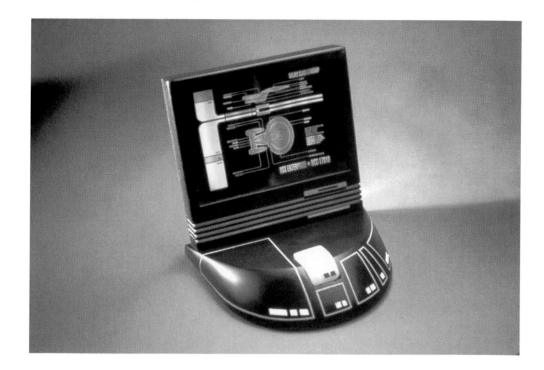

# The Mechanical Mouse

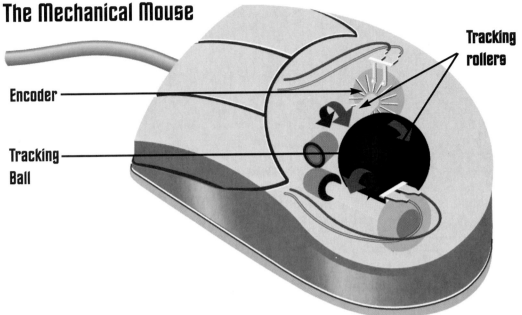

**Encoder**

**Tracking Ball**

**Tracking rollers**

Most mice were connected to the PC by means of a long electrical cord. Early designers and users noticed that the cord resembled a tail, and that the device was about the size of a small Earth creature familiar to humans as a household pest or laboratory subject. Therefore the device was called a *mouse.*

The mouse was connected to the PC through one of its ports. A *port* was an external connection for peripheral devices such as a printer, modem, or mouse. In the case of the mouse, not only was data sent through its port attachment, but electric power as well.

Moving the mechanical mouse along its mouse pad (or whatever surface the user chose), in turn rotated a rubber ball housed within it. This *tracking ball* made contact with

two tracking rollers—these rollers moved in a corresponding horizontal or vertical direction based on the movement of the tracking ball. The movement of each roller caused a small attached wheel (*encoder*) to rotate in the same direction. Attached in turn to this encoder were strips of conductive material, arranged like spokes radiating from the center.

As the wheel rotated, tiny copper brushes contacted the conductive strips on the encoders at measurable intervals, and electrical pulses were sent. The intervals between the electrical pulses indicated the speed of the mouse movement. The rotation of the rollers indicated the direction of the mouse.

A tiny switch under each of the mouse buttons recorded when a button was pressed (clicked), along with the interval between

*The program that calculated the movement and speed of the mouse was called a mouse driver, and it was loaded into memory when the PC was booted (powered up).*

each pair of clicks. All of the data concerning mouse movement was collected and sent through the "tail" (cord) to one of the PC's ports. The port passed the information to a special program loaded in memory (RAM), which calculated the movement, speed, and number of clicks from the encoded information.

The relative position of the mouse corresponded to the location of the on-screen pointer, which generally took the form of an arrow. The most common purpose of this arrow was to point to a command presented in a list, although the arrow could also assume the image of a pencil (a wooden drawing stylus). A command selection or drawing was made when one of the mouse buttons was pressed. A mouse could contain up to three buttons; their purposes were determined by the program being used. The main button was the button under the index finger (usually the left button for a right-handed user).

The act of pressing the mouse button was called *clicking* (after its characteristic noise). When the user rested the pointer on a command name or *icon* (drawing) on-screen, clicking typically activated the program, or one of its features. Pressing a mouse button twice in quick succession was called *double-clicking*. The purpose of two clicks

was often carefully distinguished from one click, even while the pointer resided over the same on-screen item. Double-clicking was often used to open a new *window* (display region), to exit a program, or to close a *selection box*.

A special method for using the mouse was called *dragging*. With this method, the user selected an on-screen object (such as a picture that represented a particular file or document), and the main button was clicked and held down as the mouse was moved. The movement of the mouse caused the on-screen pointer to move in a corresponding manner, dragging the selected object with it. When the button was released, the object was repositioned under the current pointer location.

Clicking the middle and right mouse buttons (when these were present) often served as a way to "undo" or reverse a command selected previously. Programs used these extra buttons on the mouse for their own purposes; standardized purposes were never developed.

One major problem with using a mechanical mouse was that dirt and debris would collect on the tracking ball, which occasionally had to be removed for cleaning in order for the device to work properly.

Small improvements over the original mouse design led to the *wireless mouse*, which freed the user from the constraints of the mouse and its tail (cord). A wireless mouse fed its signal to the PC through either infrared or radio signals. Infrared required an unobstructed signal path to the computer, whereas the radio signal did not. The use of wireless mice enabled a lecturer to move away from the PC while speaking to an audience. These signals were emitted whenever the mouse was moved, and received by a special box-shaped receiver attached to the computer.

# The Trackball

The trackball was simply an upside-down mouse. Rather than sliding the entire device to direct cursor movement as was done with a mechanical mouse, the trackball rested in place on a desk. Its internal rubber ball was exposed on the top-side of the trackball; it was moved with thumb and finger. The trackball had an advantage over the mouse: it did not require the space for a pad on which to run.

When the trackball was rotated by hand, it touched two rollers (motion translator axles) which rotated in a corresponding direction. Similar to the mechanics of a mouse, the direction of rotation was detected, and the appropriate signals were sent to the PC.

*"The trackball was nicknamed a "dead mouse." I find this odd, since records indicate that a trackball bore little resemblance to a lifeless furry rodent with a pointed snout, small ears, and slender tail. Nonetheless, the nickname for the device was apparently very popular".*—**Lt. Commander Data**

Trackballs usually incorporated one major improvement over their mechanical cousins: the use of LEDs (light-emitting diodes). Instead of conductive strips of material attached to wheels at the end of each roller, a slotted (perforated) *synchronizer wheel* was used, through which an LED would shine. A phototransistor on the opposite side of the wheel from the LED detected the light pulses. The changing light pulses were used to calculate the speed of the trackball's movement, along with its direction.

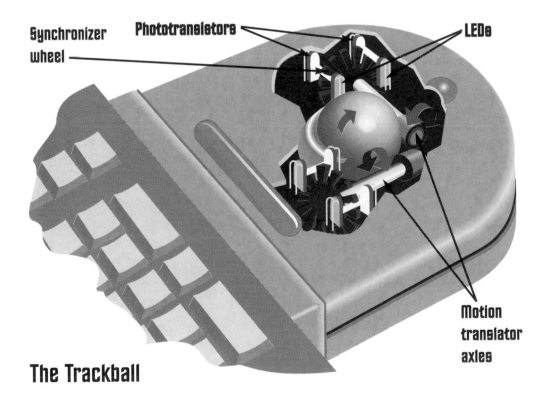

**The Trackball**

Synchronizer wheel · Phototransistors · LEDs · Motion translator axles

The majority of PC trackballs were designed to be attached to the side of keyboards, especially those belonging to portable PCs. Called *laptops*, *notebooks*, and *palmtops* (depending on their relative size), portable PCs were used in cramped spaces like the passenger seats of ancient aircraft. A present-day PADD (personal access display device) is similar in size to the palmtops used at the close of the twentieth century; however, palmtops (along with laptops and notebook PCs) were designed primarily for independent use. This is unlike a PADD, which shares its processing load with the main computer cores. A nanoprocessor within the PADD controls the uploading and downloading of data as needed, storing that information temporarily within its isolinear chips. The connection to the main computer is through a subspace transceiver assembly (STA) in an encrypted format for security reasons.

*Military engineers of Earth's 1970s pioneered development of the first trackballs for use in early radar tracking equipment, but users of these trackballs complained about their rather unwieldy design. In the mid-1970s, the United States Defense Department turned to a manufacturer of coin-operated video games, Atari, to help redesign the trackball. Trackball design from then on was based primarily on the specifications originally written for a game called "Video Football."*

*—Dr. Leah Brahms,*
*Starfleet Design Engineer*

# Graphics Tablets

The surface of a *graphics tablet* was divided into equal regions corresponding to locations on the screen. The pointing devices used with graphics tablets were *absolute* (unlike *relative* pointing devices such as the mouse or trackball), because every point on the surface of the graphics tablet was related to an exact point on the screen. This was different than using a mouse or a trackball, where the movement of the tracking ball corresponded to the relative movement of an on-screen pointer.

A graphics tablet was used with either a *stylus* or a *puck* (also called a *cursor*). A stylus was used like a "drawing pen" on the surface of the tablet; the more sophisticated ones registered minute changes in pressure at their tips, providing an adequate simulation of drawing with an actual pen or brush. The stylus was often equipped with one or more switches, designed to be used like the buttons on a mouse.

The puck or cursor resembled a mouse (and actually predated the advent of the mouse by over a decade). Among its most notable differences from a mouse was a sighting grid called a *reticle*, attached to its "nose." This transparent grid was employed in aligning the puck's position over a drawing laid upon a table. The puck was used by engineers and artists to trace complex handmade drawings; once these were digitized (converted by the graphics tablet into digital computer data), a PC could be used to modify them. The puck could also be used in place of a conventional mouse; it was equipped with similar buttons. Research reveals that the puck had been used to communicate commands to computers as far back as the early 1960s.

Regardless of which device was used (the stylus or the puck), the operating principles of each device were the same. First, the tablet would transmit an electronic signal to the pointing device. This signal produced electromagnetic resonance within the device, tuning the device to a very narrow frequency. This resonance frequency was stored temporarily in a resonant circuit.

The pointing device returned this signal at a differing frequency. The signal was received by several gridwires arranged in a crisscross pattern beneath the surface of the tablet. Here within the tablet, the exact position of the pointing device was calculated, based on the varying strength of the signal through the gridwires. The tablet converted these signals into position, switch, and pressure data, and sent this data through a cable which attached the tablet to the PC.

## Graphics Tablet

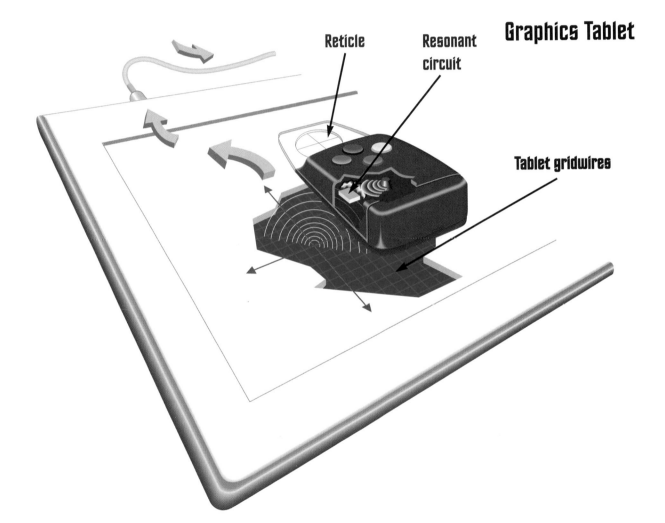

Reticle

Resonant circuit

Tablet gridwires

# Scanners

A *scanner* was a device which converted images on paper (such as documents, pictures, and artwork) into a digitized image (an image stored within a PC as binary data). There were several scanning devices whose operation varied only in the way the *scanhead* (light-sensing device) moved past the image. With a *flatbed scanner*, the image was placed face down over a plate of glass under which the scanhead moved. With an *overhead scanner*, the image was placed face up, and was scanned from above. With a *paperfeed scanner* (the type of scanner used within a *fax machine*—a device used in transmitting a printed page between locations), the image was fed through a series of rollers, which passed the image over a scanning drum. With a *hand-held scanner*, the scanning device itself was passed by hand over sections of the image until the entire image had been scanned. The resulting scans were later carefully assembled side-by-side to attain a single likeness of the entire image.

A special type of scanner, called a *bar code scanner*, was used by businesses to track inventory. The bar code (*UPC* or *Universal Package Code*) was a series of lines of varying thickness. As an item was sold, these lines were scanned, identifying the item and removing it from inventory.

Regardless of the type of scanner used, the process for digitizing the image was the same. First, a light illuminated the image. The reflected light from a single line of the image was often further reflected by a series of mirrors until it reached a lens. This lens focused the beams of light onto a sensor array which translated each beam into an electrical current. The sensor array was usually comprised of *photo diodes* (light-sensitive devices) or a *charge-coupled device* which registered the strength of the light beams and converted them into electricity.

The sensor array translated the level of the reflected light into a current of the appropriate voltage: the greater the amount of light reflection, the higher the voltage level. A special microchip called an *analog-to-digital* (or *A-D*) *converter* translated the electrical current into a digital signal (such as a byte of data). This process was repeated for each line of the image. A special program in the PC used this information to determine the amount of color (or, in a black-and-white image, the amount of grayness) in each part of the scanned image.

# Hand Scanner

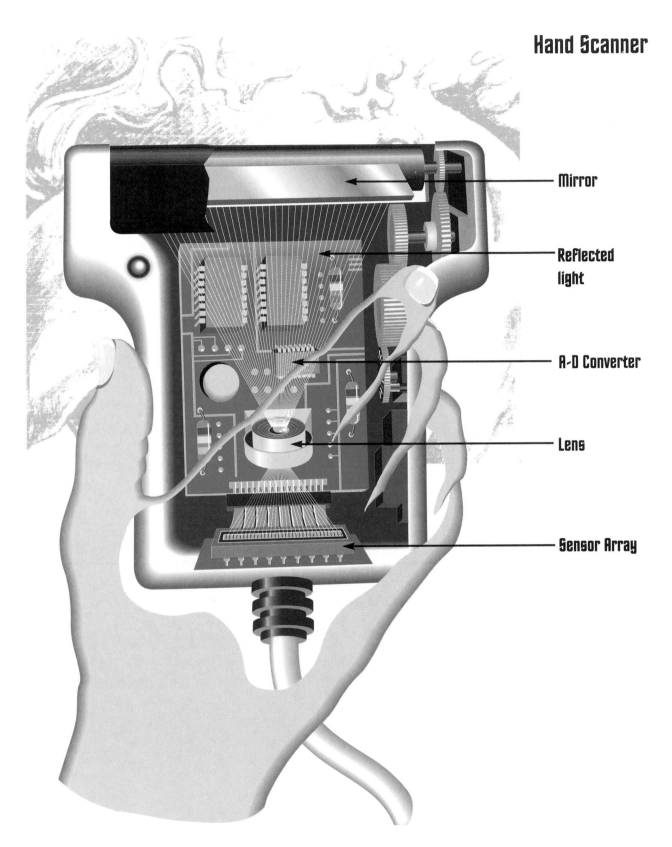

Mirror

Reflected light

A-D Converter

Lens

Sensor Array

# Touch Screens

*Touch screens* were developed in the late twentieth century primarily as simple-to-use systems that enabled users to point directly to what they wanted on-screen. When a finger touched a picture or command displayed on the screen, the general location of the fingertip on the display was detected by one of several methods. One method involved the detection of a small fluctuation in electricity at the location of the finger. In another method, the finger interrupted a series of invisible light beams passing in front of the screen's surface.

The inaccuracy of touch screens' sensors prevented them from being used for position-sensitive operations (such as creating a schematic or other drawing), though touch screens proved quite adequate for simpler operations such as command selection. A typical early touch screen was used for browsing the book collections in the large public libraries of the day.

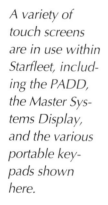

*A variety of touch screens are in use within Starfleet, including the PADD, the Master Systems Display, and the various portable keypads shown here.*

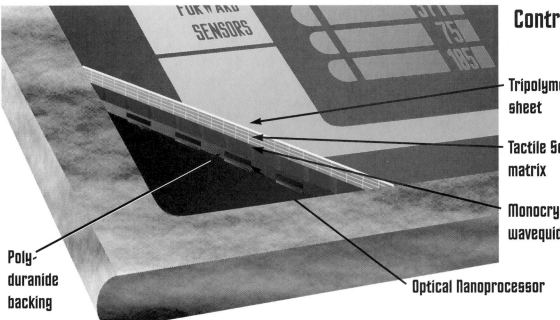

# Control Panel

Tripolymer
sheet

Tactile Sensor
matrix

Monocrystal
wavequide

Optical Nanoprocessor

Poly-
duranide
backing

The control panels in *Galaxy* class starships such as the *Enterprise* are touch-sensitive, and are made up of three layers of material. The transparent aluminum outer layer contains a sensor matrix—a series of crisscrossing electroplasmic leads that detect the press of a finger or other digit. When a user presses an area of the control panel, an embedded transducer matrix creates a slight resistance, and a confirming beep which tells the operator that the command was recognized.

Underneath the aluminum layer is an optical data crystal membrane which produces high-resolution graphical displays of varying size, dependent upon the current programmed function of the control panel. The bottom layer of the control panel consists of rugged polyduranide, which provides structural strength.

Each panel is controlled by a local processor node which connects the control panel to the ship's optical data network (ODN), which in turn provides FTL (faster-than-light) access to the central cores. Local processing (such as display and control functions) is distributed to a series of optical nanoprocessors embedded within the polyduranide layer.

Not all control panels aboard *Galaxy* class starships are programmable (multi-purpose)—some are single-purpose and especially easy to operate. For example, when new crew members or guests lose their way, the Position Finders located throughout the ship provide assistance. Constantly displayed on the Position Finder panel is a schematic of the ship, and when the panel is touched, a light is activated, indicating the user's current position. Because these particular panels are single-purpose, they have limited controls, and are therefore very simple to use.

### Touch Pads

A variation of the touch screen was the *touch pad*. This was attached to the PC through a cable, much like the mouse. Just under the surface of the touch pad were pressure-sensitive cells arranged in a grid. These cells registered the press of a finger, and translated it into an *exact* coordinate on the screen. Unlike relative pointing devices such as a mouse or a trackball, a touch pad was an *absolute* pointing device—each point on the touch pad corresponded to an exact coordinate on the screen.

# Musical Interfaces

On worlds with suitable atmospheres, sound is nearly always employed as a medium for signals, whether linguistic or musical. A pure sound is a simple sine wave ∿ —however, there are not many pure sounds in nature. Sounds are more often made up of several sine waves—which together create a unique pattern of sound. The additional waves are the *harmonics* which give each sound its unique character—for example, the harmonics of a Ferengi's voice pattern differ from those of a Klingon's. Sound—especially music—can be readily expressed as a digital pattern and saved within a computer. Once digitized, sounds can be combined, manipulated, and even incorporated into existing data files to produce a complete picture: text, pictures, and sound.

On Earth, recording sound in a digital form first became widely popular in the last two decades of the twentieth century. Digital sound was used in a variety of ways—at first in new products from the entertainment industry, and later in various occupational and educational settings (for example, to annotate documents with voice input, or to play incidental music during a presentation that utilized a PC).

A typical twentieth-century PC was equipped with a small speaker that was capable of little else but sounding warning beeps when an error occurred. To add more sophisticated sound capabilities, a *sound card* was installed in one of the expansion slots on the PC's motherboard. It was the function of the sound card to record and play back digitized sound, sometimes under the guidelines of a standard known as *MIDI* (Musical Instrument Digital Interface).

Because digitizing an actual sound was more popular than creating an artificial MIDI sound, it is the process covered here. Sound was digitized by means of a process called *sampling*. With sampling, a measurement of the audio wave was taken at regular (stepped) intervals. These measurements were plot points; when connected, they approximated the curve of the recorded audio wave. The more often a sampling (measurement) was taken, the more accurate this representation became (the smoother the curve).

*"I find the science of digitized music intriguing, although for me the use of an actual instrument is more engaging."*
—**Lt. Commander Data**

At a set sampling rate or frequency (for high-quality sound, 44.1 kHz, or every .0441 second), a sample of sound was taken. This sample was held temporarily in a special *sample-and-hold* circuit. The *amplitude* (volume of the sound in decibels) was converted to a binary number and stored in one, two, or four bytes, depending on the sound card being used.

The 16-bit (two-byte) sound cards were better able to record the exact amplitude than their 8-bit (one-byte) cousins. The 32-bit (four-byte) cards were used by professional musicians in recording studios; this digital recording method employed required more RAM and hard disk storage than general PC users could afford.

There were actually two forms in which digitized sound was saved: as *digital audio data* or as *MIDI data*. To create digital audio data, the amplitude (height) of the sound wave was measured and recorded at regular intervals. You'll learn more about this process in a moment. To create MIDI data, instructions for playing a sequence of notes was compiled. Included with these instructions were codes representing the instrument needed to produce the proper sound. MIDI was a standard that allowed instruments of varying types to communicate electronically; it was therefore favored by professional musicians for the recording of complex musical arrangements.

MIDI files were played through a *synthesizer* which used the recorded instructions to simulate the playing of acoustic instruments. MIDI technology was not designed for voice recording, since it was not concerned with the actual digital waveform—just the sequence of notes being played by a particular acoustic instrument. Because digitized sound files contained the measurement of a particular sound wave recorded at frequent intervals, they were often 10 times larger than their MIDI counterparts. However, digital technology was less expensive, and so was used more often by the general public (as opposed to professional musicians, who favored the more expensive and better-sounding MIDI technology).

Several techniques were employed during the digitizing of sound which increased the resultant quality. One technique was called *anti-aliasing*. The sound to be recorded was sent through a special filter which eliminated frequencies above 20 kHz (the upper range of human hearing). Even though these higher frequencies were not audible, when they were sent through the sampling process, they produced alias (false) frequencies within the audible range. These false frequencies produced a kind of static within the recorded sound—by eliminating them before a sampling of the sound was taken, the overall quality of the digitized sound was greatly improved. Another recording technique was called *dithering*. With dithering, random low-level background noise was added to the recorded sound prior to sampling. This background noise masked a slight clicking noise at the points in the audio wave where samples were taken.

When the recorded sound was later played, the binary data was passed through a digital-to-analog converter, where it was converted from its digital form to audio sound. This sound was held in another sample-and-hold circuit (often called an *aperture circuit*). This circuit held the converted audio sound after it passed through the digital-to-analog converter. While the sound is being held, it was passed through an *anti-imaging* filter which smoothed the edges of the stepped wave, forming a smooth curve. Finally, the sound was amplified and sent to a speaker, through which it was then heard.

*Many digitized recordings dating back to Earth's twentieth century have survived, and are stored in the Enterprise's computers, along with more recent recordings of most of the instruments used within the Federation. I do not fully understand the selection process; for example, I have located 1,248 separate digitized recordings of an ancient Earth song called, "Louie, Louie."*

*These digitized recordings provide a unique insight into the music, as well as the sociology, of that period on Earth—even when the exact meaning of the recording is not fully understood. For example, it was a habit among twentieth-century PC users to embellish their computer operations with small digitized sound effects; these usually reflected the user's personal interests. Recently, for example, a curious segment of such a digitized recording was found among the ruins of a San Jose laboratory. It contains what may be a fragment of a murder mystery—a man's voice saying, "He's dead, Jim."*

—**Lt. Commander Data**,
**Operations Manager, U.S.S. Enterprise**

# Output Devices

Twentieth-century PCs displayed their computations on monitors, or printed them on paper. Although printers are not used today, the need for "portable output" still exists. Printers (and their resultant "hard-copy printouts") have been replaced in our era by various types of personal data display pads. Since these devices have become so reliable over the years, the use of paper has grown obsolete—though I must admit to some measure of sentimentality over its disuse. There is still something romantically compelling about the crispness, the creamy texture of paper, that simply cannot be found in the cold touch of a PADD (personal access display device). Whenever I want to review particular reports in the privacy of my Ready Room, I use my desktop terminal. Perhaps the need for privacy and quiet contemplation was the ancient purpose for producing these same reports on paper.

—Captain Jean-Luc Picard, U.S.S. Enterprise

# The Monitor

The user of a twentieth-century personal computer was, for the most part, reliant upon the monitor for the instantaneous output of data. The image displayed on a typical monitor was composed of *pixels* (**pic**ture **ele**ment**s**). The display area of the monitor (the exposed portion of its picture tube) was divided into these tiny pixels. On a color monitor, the area inhabited by a pixel usually consisted of three dots—one for each of the three optical primary colors (red, green, and blue), arranged in a triangular pattern. These three dots of color were situated so closely to each other that they seemed to blend; this blending formed the bigger "circle" of the pixel. It is important to note that the pixel itself was so tiny that the user could not distinguish one pixel from another. The net effect was a blend of color in an area of the screen, formed from several pixels close together—each pixel formed from a blending of the three primary optical colors: red, green, and blue. A monitor's type determined the number of pixels that could be displayed horizontally and vertically on the monitor.

The image seen on a PC's monitor was stored in an area of memory known as *video memory*. By copying new information into this area of memory, the image on the screen could be changed. Each pixel of the display was represented in memory as a *series of bits* called a bit pattern. The number of bits required to represent a single pixel was determined by the number of possible colors used by the display—the larger the number of available colors to choose from, the larger the number of bits needed to represent each available color. The standard monitor of the late 1980s and early 1990s, VGA (Video Graphics Array), typically displayed a matrix of 640 pixels horizontally and 480 pixels vertically, in anywhere from 16 to 256 colors. Because of its wide variety of colors and high resolution (number of pixels on the display), a VGA monitor required more memory storage than existed in video memory. On a VGA monitor, the bit patterns for each pixel were assembled in another area of RAM, and then moved in and out of video memory as needed.

Control panels have the capability of displaying data within any portion of their upper surface area, complete with the three-dimensionality inherent in larger viewers such as the main viewer on the bridge of most starcraft. Embedded within the matrix of a control panel is a triaxial optical-display crystal membrane capable of producing high-resolution displays of graphics or video, within the visibility spectra of all Federation members' humanoid life forms.

If needed, special panels embedded within conference tables can project 3-D holographic images. These images can be rotated 360 degrees to accommodate any number of viewers within the conference room.

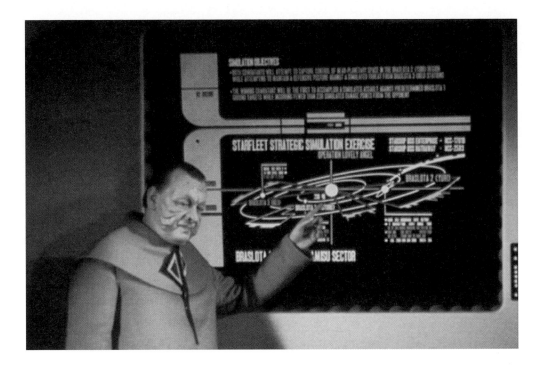

*A twenty-fourth-century display is capable of depicting all types of graphics and video.*

A character (such as the letter **d**) was represented in memory as an ASCII (American Standard Code for Information Interchange) code. Every character found on the keyboard (plus a few more) were assigned specific ASCII codes. For example, the letter **d** was assigned the code **01100100**. To display a character on the screen, a program loaded this code into the area of video memory which corresponded to the exact on-screen location at which the program wanted to display the letter **d**.

Eventually, the contents of video memory were transferred to the video controller. Prior to sending this information to the monitor for display, the video controller analyzed the information and translated any ASCII codes into a series of pixels representing the actual appearance of the character on-screen. For example, suppose (based on the current resolution of the monitor) each character on-screen was plotted within an 8-pixel-by-12-pixel grid. The video controller would then translate the ASCII code for the letter **d** into a series of 12 bytes of eight bits each. The "1" bits in each of these bytes represented a part of the displayed character—a pixel to be turned "on." A "0" within the grid would represent on "off" pixel. When all of these "on" and "off" pixels were placed side by side on the screen, they formed the letter d.

Graphics differed from text in their manner of display. While every text character was assigned a specific code, there were no codes for graphic objects such as trees or spheres. To store a graphic image in RAM, it was necessary to create a *bit map*—a series of bits coded as either "on" or "off." Each individual bit was associated with a pixel (dot) of the image to be displayed.

*The patterns for each character were stored in a special ROM chip called character ROM. In order to translate the ASCII codes, the video controller simply requested the correct pattern from character ROM.*

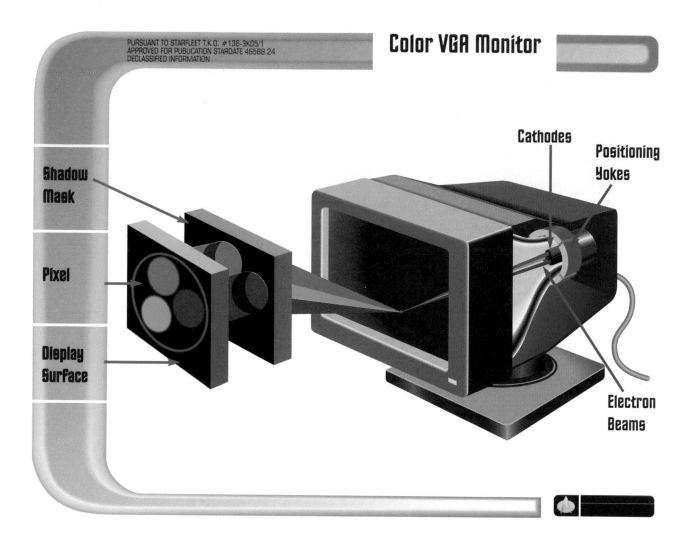

PURSUANT TO STARFLEET T.K.O. #136-3K05/1
APPROVED FOR PUBLICATION STARDATE 46588.24
DECLASSIFIED INFORMATION

**Color VGA Monitor**

Shadow Mask

Pixel

Display Surface

Cathodes

Positioning Yokes

Electron Beams

Once the proper information was stored in video memory, it was transferred to the screen in several steps. First, the first line of the display was transferred from RAM to the video controller. This information was converted to electrical pulses by a series of *digital-to-analog converters* (DACs). Additional control information was added, and the stream of electrical pulses was then sent to the monitor.

Within the monitor were three *cathodes* (electron emitters), each representing one of the three optical primary colors: blue, red, and green. The electrical pulses received from the video controller caused each cathode to emit a stream of electrons of varying intensity. For each pixel, the varying intensity levels of all three cathodes combined to create a dot of unique color on the display.

The video data was transferred from RAM to the video controller using either the main bus, or the local video bus. Using the main bus, data was transferred to the video controller at the data width of the expansion bus slots—if the video controller was plugged into an ISA expansion bus slot, data was transferred in 16-bit units, regardless of the transfer speed (data width) of the local CPU.

The local bus connected the video controller directly to the CPU, allowing data to travel over that bus at the CPU's own speed (60 MHz or better) and data width (usually 32 to 64 bits). Using a local video bus eliminated the problem of moving data to the monitor at the same slow speed used for every other PC component. The first PCs contained local video buses, though the use of this bus became widely discontinued for a time, as developers of certain monitors produced systems that literally overrode the PC's local video bus. The result of this sidestepping process, at first, was displays with higher resolution and greater display speed. However, when the technical specifications of these monitors become standardized, it suddenly became economically and technically feasible once again for PC manufacturers to use local buses for video.

These three electron beams were focused through a hole in a metal plate called a *shadow mask*. This hole was aligned with the position of a pixel on the screen. The interior surface of the monitor was painted at various points with three different phosphorous compounds—each of which, when energized by the electron beams, glowed a different color: blue, red, and green. The shadow mask focused the three beams so that each beam struck the phosphorus compound to which it was related. For example, after passing through the tight control of the shadow mask, the red beam would strike only the red phosphorus compound within a single pixel. The electron beams that passed through the shadow mask struck this phosphorescent surface, causing three individual dots of phosphor to glow. The visible glow produced by the phosphor corresponded (in color frequency and intensity) to the intensity of the beam.

*Horizontal yokes* on either side of the cathodes made minute adjustments to the magnetic field surrounding the beams, causing them to focus on the next pixel. Each pixel was lit in turn, completing a single horizontal sweep (the first line) of the display. Meanwhile, the series of bytes representing the second line of the display was being transferred from RAM to the video controller, where it was converted into electrical pulses and forwarded to the monitor.

On a twenty-fourth-century display, realistic three-dimensional images are made possible through the use of a special depth-sensitive display matrix. The crystals which compose the display membranes of control panels are triaxial, a property which gives the crystals the ability to display images in three dimensions for the benefit of binoptical life forms such as humanoids.

# Printers

*Three-dimensional images can be displayed on the main viewer, and on most display panels.*

Inside the monitor, as one horizontal sweep was completed, the electron beams were temporarily shut off. A quick adjustment in the *horizontal yoke* caused the beams to sweep back to the left side of the screen; a minor adjustment of the *vertical yoke* caused them to refocus on the next scan line down the length of the display. Once focused, the beams were turned on, and another horizontal sweep was begun. The electron beams followed a tight zig-zag pattern—beginning in the upper left corner of the display and moving toward the bottom right—eventually covering every pixel on the display. The phosphors would continue to glow for a brief period of time, during which the electron beams repeated another sweep of the entire display, refreshing each pixel about 60 times per second. This screen-sweeping process went unseen by the user of the PC, to whom the display appeared relatively solid and unfluxuating.

PC users often reviewed their computer data by transferring it onto paper, a process known as "making a *hard copy*." The device used to create hard copy was called a *printer*. PCs employed various types of printers, each of which differed in the method used for depositing tiny dots of ink (or some such pigment) onto paper. Printers fell into two major categories: *impact printers* (which used metal pins to press ink onto paper) and *non-impact printers* (whose methods varied—some heated an inked roller and pressed it against the paper, others dropped or squirted the ink onto the paper). The two most popular types of impact and non-impact printers were, respectively, *dot-matrix* and *laser*.

Regardless of the type of printer employed, the methods the PC used for printing a character began in the same way: the character to be printed was represented in memory by its ASCII code value. (For the letter **d**, as you will recall, this code was 01100100.) If the program wanted to print a graphic image instead, a *bit map* (a series of bits coded as either "on" or "off") formed the pattern of the image to be printed.

Some printers used another method to print characters on paper. Instead of using a specific ASCII code for a character, the computer would send the printer a series of mathematical formulas. A common language employed to represent these formulas was called *PostScript*. The formulas described the exact placement of lines and curves needed to create a letter or other characters. In order to use these formulas, a printer was equipped with additional programs to translate the PostScript instructions into the proper pattern of dots. An alternative method involved having an intermediary program within the computer translate the instructions and send the translation data to the printer.

In addition to text and graphic images, the PC's current program added codes that told the printer when to move to the next line on the paper, or the next page. When all this data was compiled, that program loaded it into RAM and sent an interrupt to the CPU. An interrupt, you may recall, was a signal that a program sent to the CPU in order to get its attention. The CPU passed this particular interrupt to ROM BIOS, because the

BIOS contained the instructions for passing data to and from a computer's peripherals, such as the printer. ROM BIOS processed the request to print by transferring the contents of the specified area of RAM to the printer port. Ports were special connections that allowed information to enter and leave the system unit. The printer port (usually a *parallel port*) forwarded the data to the printer via a cable.

Just as it would be impractical for a twentieth century architect to return to his or her office every time he or she needed to refer to building plans, one cannot expect every starship crew member to return to his or her terminal to verify some data. The PADD (personal access display device) provides a "hard copy" wherever it may be needed. Similar to control panels (but unlike twentieth-century paper printouts), the PADD contains a three-dimensional display.

*Parallel ports transferred data through parallel wires, one byte (eight bits) at a time.*

*The PADD allows users to carry reports and other data with them.*

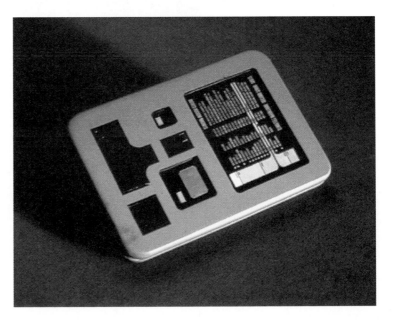

## Dot-Matrix Printers

One major disadvantage to using dot-matrix printers was the noise they made—the sound of the pins smashing the inked ribbon against the paper, at an average of 75 decibels, exceeded the threshold of normal background noise by a considerable margin. A colleague of mine who runs a museum showed me one of these early printer devices she had restored, and after hearing it work, I must say it's a wonder that human hearing ever survived the twentieth century.

—*Dr. Kate Pulaski,*
*M.D., Starfleet*
*Medical*

By the end of the 1900s, dot-matrix was by far the most popular and widely-employed type of printer. Although its relatively simple technology did not provide the best quality of *output* (printed page), dot-matrix printers were consistently less expensive to use, and their output quality was more than adequate for most purposes.

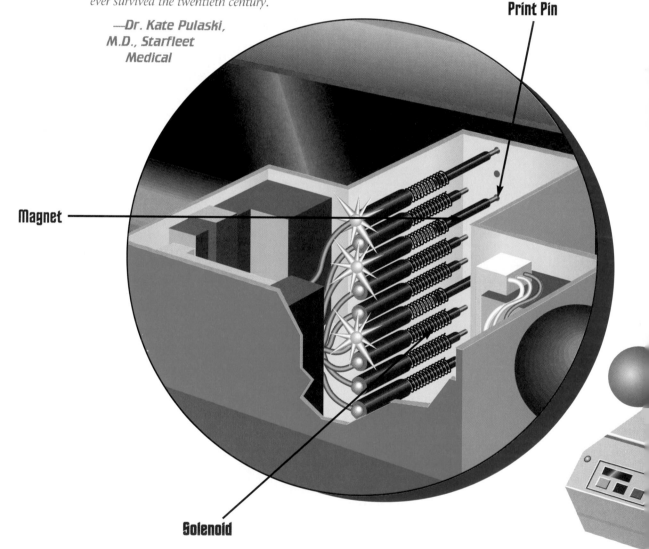

**Print Pin**

**Magnet**

**Solenoid**

A dot-matrix printer worked in the following manner: first, data was sent to the printer through a cable which connected it to the PC. The arriving data was stored temporarily in a *printer buffer*, where it awaited processing. The printer's CPU separated the *printer data* (the actual information to be printed) from the *printer instructions*. One of these instructions told the printer's *imaging program* which of several internal tables to use when translating characters. Using the proper bitmap table, the imaging program translated any ASCII characters into a bitmap pattern with a particular *font* (a term inherited from the ancient printing trade, meaning a particular typeface style). The resulting bitmaps were stored in the printer's memory until an entire line of print was assembled.

With the printer data translated and in memory, the print engine program used the assembled data to send a series of electrical pulses to the *print head*. In a dot-matrix printer, the print head contained either nine or 24 *print pins*. If nine pins were used,

they were arranged in a single vertical line. If 24 pins were used, they were arranged in two vertical columns.

Each of these print pins was held in place by a *solenoid* (a coil of wire that, when energized, produces a magnetic field). When an electrical pulse was sent to a specific solenoid, the magnetic field it created repelled a magnet inside the coil, propelling the magnet forward. The print pin, located at the end of the magnet, was propelled toward the paper, striking an ink-coated ribbon. The ribbon left a dot of ink on the paper at the exact position where it was struck by the print pin. The electrical pulse was shut off, causing the magnetic field of the solenoid to fade. With nothing to repel it, the magnet attached to the print pin pulled the print pin back into position for the next row of dots.

The print engine program continued to send electrical pulses to the print head until an entire line of characters was printed. The print engine sent instructions to the *platen* (a roller which guided the paper through the printer) to advance the paper one line. Speeds varied by printer, but to print one line of text usually took about a half a second.

*A dot-matrix print head that used 24 pins was capable of producing higher quality output than a print head that used only nine pins.*

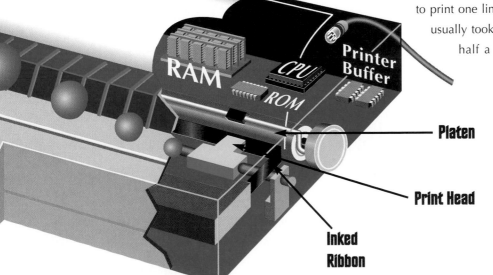

Platen

Print Head

Inked Ribbon

## Laser Printers

Laser printers were prized for their high-quality output. A laser printer worked in the following manner: first (as with a dot-matrix printer) data was sent to the printer through a cable which connected it to the PC. The arriving data was stored temporarily in a printer buffer where it awaited processing.

The printer's CPU separated the printer instructions from the printer data. Next, the printer's imaging program processed the printer data, assembling the image of an entire page and storing it in the printer's memory.

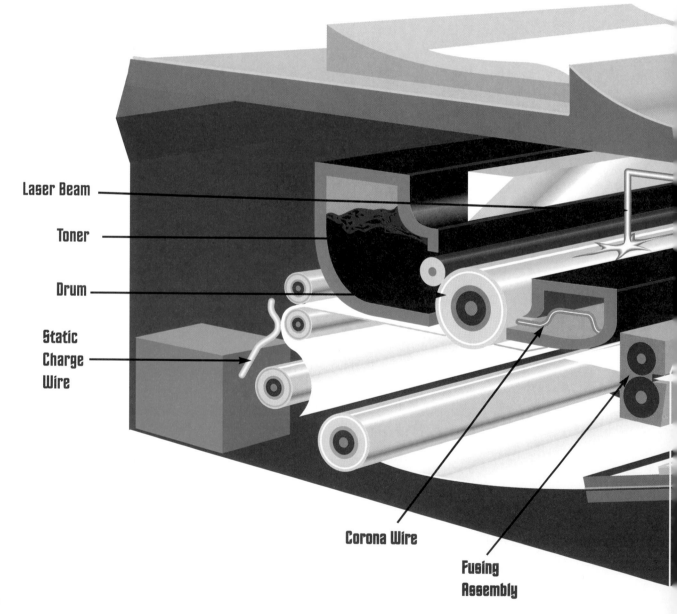

Laser Beam

Toner

Drum

Static
Charge
Wire

Corona Wire

Fusing
Assembly

With the printer data translated and in memory, the printer's CPU called the print engine program. Instead of an electromechanical print head, however, the print engine program controlled a weak laser beam and a series of mirrors. Using the assembled page data in printer memory, the print engine program sent signals to fire the laser beam. A mirror

deflected the beam, causing it to strike an electrostatically-charged roller (*drum*).

The print engine program continued to fire the laser beam, adjusting the mirror so that the beam struck the drum in various places along a horizontal line. After sweeping the drum horizontally, the laser would then move down a fraction of a centimeter to the next horizontal line. The beam produced by the laser was switched on and off many times during the sweep process, leaving a pattern of charged points on the surface of the drum. This pattern formed a reverse image of the page to be printed.

Next, the drum rolled through a cloud of tiny magnetized *toner* (ink) particles. These black, dust-like particles were attracted to those charged points where the laser beam had struck; they clung to the drum, making the reverse image appear in magnetic ink. As the drum continued to roll, a piece of paper was passed beneath it. Between the drum and the paper was an electrically-charged wire. The wire caused the paper passing under it to accumulate a slight static charge. The static charge of the paper pulled the toner (ink) dust off the drum and onto the paper, leaving a printed image on the page.

The paper continued to travel along rollers until it reached the *fusing assembly*, which heated the page, binding the toner dust permanently to the paper. The drum, meanwhile, continued to roll, passing another charged wire called the *corona wire*, which neutralized the charges left by the laser beams. The drum was now prepared to receive the image of the next page to be printed.

*During most of the twentieth-century paper was considered the most reliable storage medium of the time. Later, as their reliablity was proven, electronic—and then holographic—data-encoding replaced paper as the favored storage medium. Even though paper itself is no longer manufactured, I think it's interesting that the term "paper work" has not fallen out of use. (I sometimes wish it had!)*

**—Deanna Troi, Counselor,**
**U.S.S. Enterprise**

# Chapter Six

# Storage Devices

*The permanent storage media of the twentieth century were relatively slow compared to the fast access times of today's isolinear chips. However, hard disk drives were a remarkably reliable technology for their day. Although magnetic media were limited by their very nature, engineers of the twentieth century displayed remarkable ingenuity by improving both access times and storage capacities year after year—until magnetic media were eventually rendered obsolete by more efficient units.*

—Lt. Commander Geordi La Forge, Chief of Engineering, U.S.S. Enterprise

# Hard Disk Drives

PCs recorded most of their data on magnetic disks. Large storage needs (amounts over 1 or 2 megabytes) were met by *hard disk drives* that were typically mounted permanently inside a PC's system unit. Removable hard disks, utilizing a slightly different magnetic recording technology, were sometimes employed as a security measure—these hard disks could be removed from the system unit and locked in a safe place until the data they contained was needed. Smaller amounts of data were often recorded on *floppy diskettes*, which employed a magnetic technology similar to that of hard disk drives. Unlike most hard disks, floppy diskettes were removeable from their drives—making them an excellent choice for the transportation of data from one system to another.

The first hard drives were capable of little more than a dozen megabytes of storage. By the end of the century, however, typical hard disk drives had an average capacity of 20 gigabytes. (A gigabyte was equal to 1,000 megabytes.) All types of permanent data were stored on hard disk drives, including a PC's programs, operating system, and data files. (You will learn more about the role of programs and the PC operating system in later chapters.)

*A cluster could contain from 2 to 16 sectors, depending on the limitations of the PC's disk operating system.*

Although referred to in the singular ("hard disk"), the drive actually contained several disks called *platters*. Covered with a magnetic alloy, these platters were suspended within 3 to 4 millimeters of each other in a stack inside the drive. They rotated as a unit on the *spindle*. Above each platter in the stack floated a *read/write head*, a magnetically-sensitive device which transferred data to and from the platter without actually touching it. A servo motor adjusted the position of the head along the diameter of the platter. You will learn more about the processes involved in recording data to a hard disk later in this section.

The first PCs did not contain a hard disk—they had yet to be miniaturized. Interestingly enough, hard disk technology had existed for several years—they were employed as the main storage media used in large mainframe computers. Until the advent of portable computers, the need for smaller hard disks did not yet exist. So these early PCs recorded their permanent data onto floppy diskettes. Because they did not have the storage capacities of hard disks at their disposal, these PCs were forced to rely on simple, small programs which could be copied onto a handful of diskettes. Even the PC's *operating system* (main command program) was copied from a diskette when the PC was first booted (started).

Data was written to the hard disk in concentric circles called *tracks*. Each track was divided into equal segments called *sectors*. Several sectors together formed a *cluster*, the smallest increment of mass data storage. Tracks and sectors were established magnetically during a one-time process called *formatting*, which prepared a new disk for use.

The user of a PC generally was not aware of the existence of tracks, sectors, and clusters. From the user's viewpoint, it appeared as if files were saved in a single location somewhere on the hard disk. In actuality, files larger than a single cluster were divided among several available clusters, using the hard disk's internal map (File Allocation Table). The FAT was a record of files stored on the hard disk; it also showed the locations of unused clusters. No matter how small the file, it occupied at least one entire cluster. A sector stored 512 bytes of data; if a cluster for a particular hard drive was defined as 4 sectors, each file would consume 2,048 bytes (2 kilobytes) of hard disk space at minimum. Therefore, a small file consisting of only a few bytes would waste most of the two kilobytes apportioned

it. Statistical averages compiled by scientists of the day showed that, on average, each file wasted one-half cluster of a hard disk's space.

Other storage inefficiencies affected the computer's performance more directly. As files were deleted from the hard disk because they were no longer needed—or, as was common in that day, by accident—the clusters they occupied became available for use by other files. As files were added and deleted over time, these clusters became pockets of available space scattered throughout the hard disk. When a file in RAM was to be stored on the disk, DOS searched for available space. Upon finding the first free pocket—regardless of its size—DOS would begin writing the file there. After running out of space, DOS would continue writing the

*If a file was stored in several clusters, the first cluster location was recorded in the FAT. A pointer, stored with each cluster, led the operating system to the next cluster in the chain.*

The primary storage area of a starship's main computer system is called *core memory*. Its optical method of storage has an average access time of 4,600 kiloquads per second—well suited to the rapidly-changing situations of travel at warp speed. Though its magnetically-based storage was slower, hard disk technology of the twentieth century was well suited to its time, with data transfer rates expressed in millions—as *megabits per second* (mbps) or *megabytes per second* (M/sec, one-eighth the mbps rate).

Various hard disk technologies offered differing transfer rates: the ESDI (Enhanced **S**mall **D**evice **I**nterface) standard transferred data at rates that ranged from 1.25 to 3.124 M/sec. The AT Attachment Interface improved on this figure (at 4 to 8 M/sec), and SCSI (**S**mall **C**omputer **S**ystem **I**nterface) achieved even better transfer rates at 8 to 40 M/sec. These average speeds varied by PC, depending on two factors: the speed of the computer's internal bus (see Chapter 2 for a review), and the presence of performance-enhancing technologies (such as *track buffering* and *disk caching*, described later in this chapter).

file in the next available pocket. As a result, new data files were stored in non-sequential clusters scattered around the disk—a condition called *fragmentation*. When this condition occurred, additional time was needed to find each part of a scattered file—more than it would take if the file were stored in consecutive sectors.

As fragmentation increased, the hard disk required more and more time to read and write the same amount of data. Periodically, to restore peak performance, the user would run special *utility* programs which rearranged the pieces of a file onto consecutive clusters on the disk. With time, however, fragmentation would begin anew, forcing the user to eventually rerun the defragmentation utility. Such conditions were characteristic of this early period in Earth's computer development when users were obliged to perform much of their computers' file maintenance.

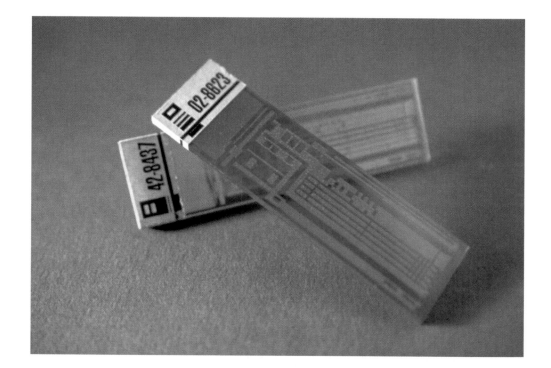

Isolinear chips are the primary medium for data storage—both permanent and temporary—inside twenty-fourth-century computer cores. These versatile storage devices employ holographic optical storage technology; data is written to the isolinear chip in standard holographic format, using a low-density laser beam. Just as tiny changes in magnetic polarity were used to store data on twentieth-century hard disks, isolinear chips store data through subatomic changes in their cystalline structure. Because of the coercivity of its optical crystal structure, data stored on an isolinear chip does not fade with time. An internal nanoprocessor performs data configuration and storage activities for each isolinear chip, optimizing data access by the computer core.

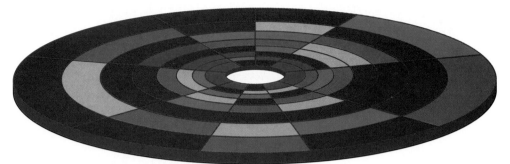

**Fragmented Drive**

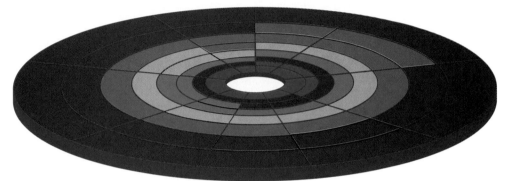

**Defragmented Drive**

The second version of the Microsoft Disk Operating System (DOS) was, in fact, the *first* to recognize the presence of a hard disk drive within the PC. The second and third versions of DOS (known informally as DOS 2 and DOS 3) set logical limits on the size of a drive. They could map *no more than 32 megabytes* of data on a single drive—primarily because the designers of the operating systems felt the user would never require more than 32 megabytes.

Manufacturers of hard disk drives ignored such limitations. To suit the demands of customers, they built hard disks whose capacities exceeded 32 MB. If a PC was equipped with one of these larger hard disks, it could still be used under DOS 3 by assigning it multiple maps, or *logical drives*, of 32 megabytes apiece or less. In later versions of DOS (beginning with version 4.0), the standard disk-allocation maps were revised to change the 32-megabyte limit. The storage map for a single logical drive was apportioned a maximum of 128 megabytes under DOS version 4, 512 megabytes under DOS 5, and 2048 megabytes under DOS 6.

# How Information Was Saved to a Hard Disk

While a user was making changes to a file or creating a new one, that file was stored temporarily in RAM (memory). When the user issued a command to save the file permanently to the PC's hard drive, the following

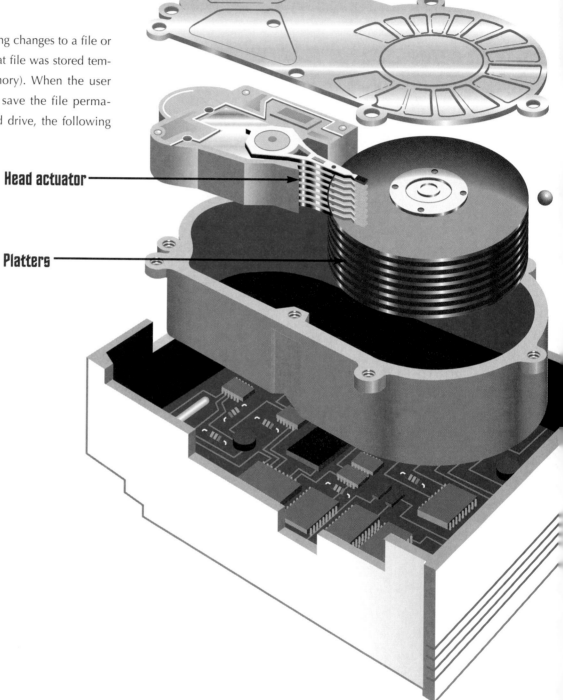

Head actuator

Platters

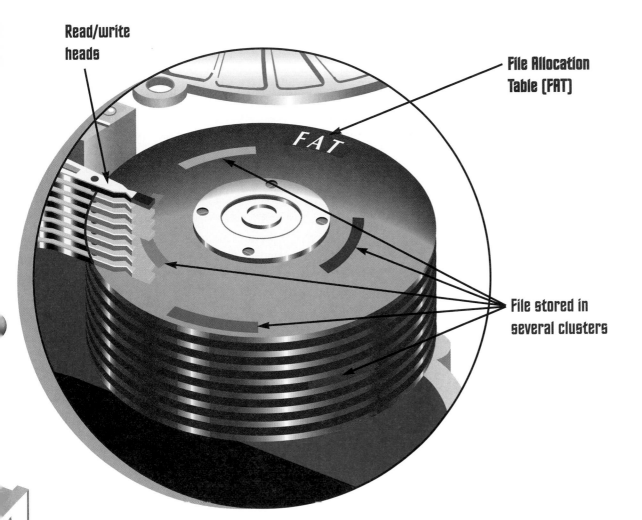

**Read/write heads**

**File Allocation Table (FAT)**

**File stored in several clusters**

*FAT*

steps occurred: first, a command was sent to the disk drive controller, requesting the current contents of the file allocation table (FAT). The FAT contained the location of the clusters occupied by existing files. Using this information, the disk operating system (DOS) located an appropriate number of available clusters in which to store the file.

The file's data was then sent to the disk drive controller, along with instructions for distributing the file on the disk (which clusters to allocate). The controller converted the cluster-allocation instructions into electrical pulses, and sent them to the *head actuator*. In response, the head acutator moved the read/write heads so that one of the heads

*Although the FAT was itself stored on the hard drive, DOS did not consider it a file.*

was directly over the first cluster to be used in storing the file. Once the read/write head was in place, it used a magnetic pulse to realign the particles on the surface of the platter. Based on the alignment of these magnetic particles, a pattern representing the file's contents was formed. Later, when the file's contents were needed, the read/write head scanned the alignment of these particles, and translated them into electrical on-and-off pulses that represented "1s" and "0s" to the computer.

The head actuator continued to move the read/write heads over the platters, storing individual clusters of data, until the entire file was saved to the hard disk. A final pulse to the head acutator moved the read/write heads back to the file allocation table, where it recorded the locations of the file's clusters.

Although most hard disks were *fixed* (installed permanently inside the system unit), some hard disks were removable. Removable hard disks contained platters sealed within in a protective plastic cartridge (rather than the almost air-tight metal container of the fixed hard disk drive). The cartridge of removable hard disks separated the platters from the solid-state components of the drive unit, which always remained permanently connected to the structure of the PC. An aperture in the removable cartridge allowed the read/write heads access to the platters, though this same aperture also permitted airborne contaminants to damage the magnetic data over time. Later improvements in removable hard disk technology decreased this risk by encasing the entire drive head mechanism with the platters.

The components of a stored file were often scattered among several clusters on the hard disk. These clusters, although not in consecutive locations, were often located on the same track. One improvement in the hard disks of the 1990s was a system called *track buffering,* which accelerated the reading process. After locating the first cluster for a file, the entire track containing that cluster was then read into in a special memory area called the *track buffer.* From there, it was an easy process to read any additional clusters within that same track. Reading data from memory (a solid-state component) was always faster than to read that same data from the hard disk (a component with lots of moving parts). Track buffering used this advantage, as did a process called *disk caching.*

Disk caching took advantage of the fact that the same files were often requested by a program again and again. With disk caching, as files were read from the hard disk, a designated number of nearby clusters would be copied (along with the requested files) to memory. This special memory was known as the *disk cache,* and it was located either in RAM or a dedicated block of memory in the disk drive controller. As the cache filled, the oldest file in it was overwritten by a newer file. When a request for a file was made, a quick scan of the disk cache was performed. If the file had been used recently, it was likely to be found within the cache. Such a file could be read quickly, without accessing the hard disk directly. Track buffering and cacheing were techniques which were employed to increase read/write speed in other areas, not just hard disks.

# Diskettes and Floppy Disk Drives

*The magnetic disks inside diskette casings were indeed flexible, but the ancient term "floppy diskette" seems misleading. Clearly the diskettes were not designed to flop while in operation. Moreover, when I have experimented with "flopping" one of the smaller 3 1/2" floppy diskettes, I found them not to be floppy at all. Indeed, several of my test specimens shattered rather than flopped. I find "diskette" a more precise term, though scholars still use "floppy disk drive" to refer to the drives.*

**—Lt. Commander Data, Operations Manager, U.S.S. Enterprise**

Before the advent of hard disk drives for PCs, *diskettes* were the primary data storage medium for the personal computer. Later, diskettes became a useful secondary backup to the primary copies of files stored on hard disks. As with hard disks, the data on diskettes was arranged magnetically in tracks and sectors. Diskettes acquired their informal name—"floppy diskettes"—because of the flexible magnetic medium they used—a mylar film coated with a thin layer of magnetic oxide. Diskettes differed from hard disks in another important way: they were designed to be removed from the PC, permitting data transport from system to system.

Diskettes were primarily manufactured in two sizes. Diskettes were measured by the circumference of the magnetic disk inside: 5.25 inches or 3.5 inches (an earlier size, 8 inches in circumference, quickly fell out of use as floppy disk drives were miniaturized). The sleeve protecting the 5.25-inch disk was also flexible; the 3.5-inch disk, in its more

durable polyurethane shell, was better protected. Each size of diskette was designed to fit into a correspondingly sized floppy disk drive. To maintain full compatibility with all diskette media, PCs of the day often contained a floppy disk drive of each size.

> The isolinear chip easily meets the permanent storage needs of the twenty-fourth century, while also providing a convenient, portable storage medium. Modeled after earlier crystal memory cards, portable isolinear chips provide large storage capacities in a small format. In order to make isolinear chips more rugged and therefore suitable for transportation between computer systems, they are sealed. The application of a tripolymer sealant protects the isolinear chip's refractive surface, protecting the holographic patterning from airborne contaminants. Several Starfleet devices provide for portable storage on isolinear chips, including optical chip readers, tricorders, and PADDs.

The density of a diskette determined the amount of data it was capable of storing—the higher the density, the more storage was available. Most diskettes were manufactured in two standard types: *double-density* and *high-density*. High-density diskettes contained at least twice as much data as their double-density counterparts. Although two diskettes were of similar size, they might have different densities. The density of a diskette was determined by the *density of the magnetic particles* scattered throughout the oxide material of the magnetic film they contained.

*An inch was an ancient unit of measurement whose name derives from a Latin phrase meaning "twelfth." In the sixteenth-century on Earth, the length of an inch was determined to be one-twelfth the average length of the feet of European male farmers from toe to heel: approximately 2.54 centimeters.*

*One of the more interesting diskette formats uncovered during my research was called extra-density. These diskettes used a dense magnetic medium that required two heads to read or write data. Because of the difficulty in manufacturing extra-density diskettes and drives, they were never very popular, and they were soon eclipsed by more advanced recording media.*
**—Lt. Commander Data**

notch on one side of the diskette was covered by a small piece of tape (a urethane band coated with adhesive). This tab could be removed later if the user wished to erase or reuse the diskette. A 5.25-inch floppy disk drive contained a sensor which detected when this notch was covered, causing the drive to refuse commands to write data onto the diskette. To write-protect a 3.5-inch diskette, a small plastic tab was pushed up, revealing a square hole. When the sensor detected a light shining through the hole, the drive refused all commands to write data onto the diskette.

A *write-protect* notch or tab protected the data on a diskette against accidental erasure. To "write-protect" a 5.25-inch diskette, a

# 3.5-inch Floppy Disk Drive

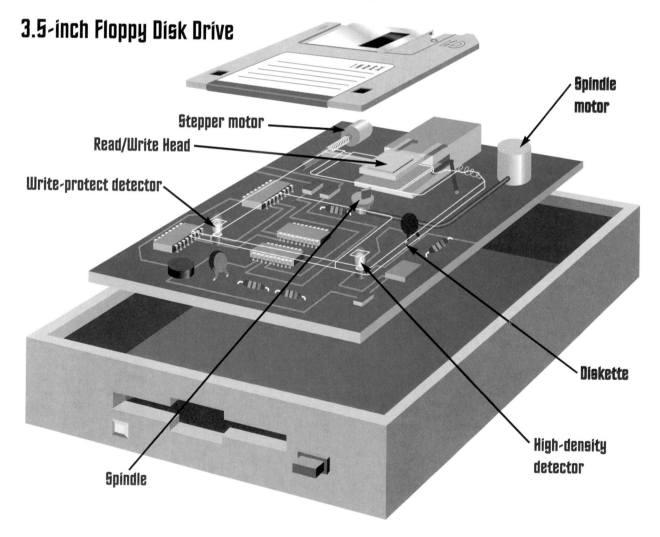

Stepper motor

Read/Write Head

Write-protect detector

Spindle motor

Diskette

High-density detector

Spindle

All floppy disk drives were operated in a similar manner: first, the diskette was placed in its drive, label side up. When a 3.5-inch diskette was inserted into its drive, a spring-loaded metal plate (called the *shutter*) was slid to one side. This revealed the magnetic mylar film inside the casing. Then a hook attached to a spindle motor made contact with a precisely-located hole on the underside of the diskette hub. Once it was hooked, the spindle motor began spinning the mylar disk.

Next, the floppy disk drive controller received a signal from the PC's CPU, indicating whether this was a read or a write operation, and the clusters involved. Meanwhile, a *LED* (*light-emitting diode*) located near the diskette's write-protect tab determined whether the drive controller should be permitted to write data onto the diskette. A similar LED located near the high-density indicator determined the diskette's density. (A high-density diskette contained a perforation (hole) at this location.)

Next, a signal was sent to the stepper motor to move the read/write head to the appropriate track and sector for the *read* or *write operation*. To read the contents of a diskette, the read/write head determined the polarization of the magnetic particles for each bit within a cluster, and translated them into electrical pulses. The presence of an electrical pulse was equivalent to a 1 bit; its absence was equivalent to a 0 bit. To write

data to a diskette, the drive controller sent electrical pulses through the read/write head, which issued a corresponding magnetic pulse. By changing the polarity of individual magnetic particles on the surface of the diskette, the 1 and 0 bits of data could be written.

# CD-ROM

Unlike hard and floppy disks' which stored data magnetically, the data on *compact disc-read only memory* (*CD-ROM*) was stored and retrieved *optically*. Data was etched permanently onto a compact disc by a laser; it could not be erased. The first CD-ROM drives could only read data from the compact disc, though later drives allowed the user to write data onto the CD—once and once only, never to be erased. CD-ROMs were the perfect medium for distributing large amounts of permanent data such as software (programs), electronic publishing, and multimedia tutorials (a combination of sound, animation, video, graphics, and data—the forerunner of the Federation's remote schooling program).

*In deference to the Norwegian company that invented CD technology, the term "compact disc" was generally spelled with a "c" rather than with a "k."*

Early experiments in optical data technology (such as CD-ROM) led to the development of crystal memory cards, and eventually to the isolinear chip. Although the technologies involved are different, a study of early optical data storage media is worthwhile.

*A holographic reader is used to access data within an isolinear chip.*

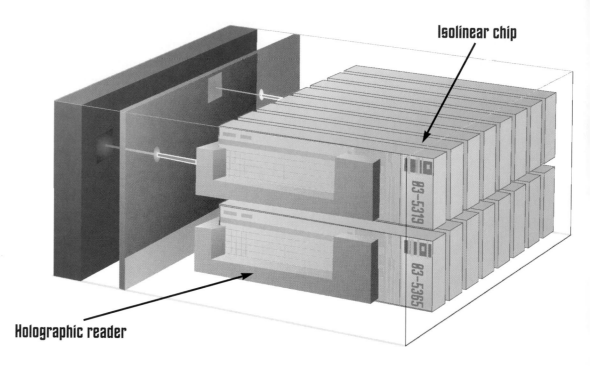

**Isolinear chip**

**Holographic reader**

A compact disc was composed of polycarbonate plastic, coated with a thin layer of aluminum (then a highly reflective metal, unlike the transparent type of aluminum so familiar aboard starships). A lacquer overcoating kept the aluminum surface free from dust and contamination. A silk-screened label was often applied to one side of the disc, identifying its contents. Data was stored as *pits* (indentations) and *lands* (bumps) on the reflective aluminum surface of the CD-ROM. A pit (indentation) reflected less light than a land (bump). A photo detector in the CD-ROM drive measured the reflected light and translated the pits and lands into the 1's and 0's of binary computer data.

Instead of storing data in concentric tracks (like magnetic media), the data on a CD-ROM was stored in a single track which spiraled outward from the center of the disc. Files were stored in consecutive sectors on this single track. The technology involved allowed data on a CD-ROM to be arranged more densely than on hard or floppy disks (16,000 "tracks" per inch, compared to 96 tracks on the average diskette).

Unlike a hard or floppy disk drive, a CD-ROM drive rotated its disc at a variable rate: as data was read from the outer edge of the disc, the disc was rotated more slowly. As data was read from the center of the disc, the disc was rotated at a faster rate. Data was packed more densely at the outer edge of the CD, so by varying the spin rate of the disc, data was read from the disc at a constant rate.

When data was read from a CD-ROM, the address of the file was sent to the CD-ROM drive controller. The controller sent a signal to the gallium-arsenide *laser*, which emitted its beam. The laser beam passed through a *diffraction plate*, which added two small beams on either side of the main beam— these side beams were used to calibrate the speed of the disc. Next, the beams passed through a *collimating lens*, which forced the beams to travel in parallel.

The beams then traveled through a *quarter-wave plate* which changed their polarity by ninety degrees. After that, they struck a prism from which they traveled upward to the CD-ROM disc. Next, the beams passed through an *objective lens* and the protective plastic surface of the CD-ROM, where their focus was tightened. Finally, the beams struck the aluminum inner surface of the CD-ROM.

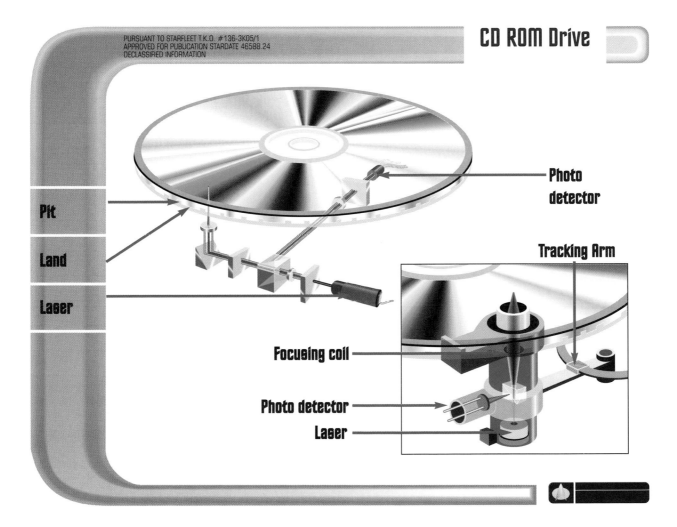

PURSUANT TO STARFLEET T.K.O. #136-3K05/1
APPROVED FOR PUBLICATION STARDATE 46588.24
DECLASSIFIED INFORMATION

**CD ROM Drive**

Photo detector

Pit

Land

Laser

Tracking Arm

Focusing coil

Photo detector

Laser

As the light struck the aluminum surface, it was reflected back to the optical reading head. If the light struck a pit, less light was reflected; if the light struck a land, more light was reflected. A prism bent this reflected light toward a photodetector which measured its strength and converted it into alternating pulses of electricity. The CD-ROM controller passed these signals (which represented binary data) to the PC's CPU for processing.

In an alternative drive design, the laser was placed perpendicular to the CD-ROM's surface. The laser beam passed through fewer lenses in this design—instead of a series of lenses, an *electromagnetic focusing coil* focused the laser beam. Also, in this design, a tracking arm moved the read/write head radially across the disc's surface. (In the more common design, the read/write head traveled on a mechanical sled.)

Data is stored within an isolinear chip in Euclidean space as a holographic image. When data is requested, LCARS determines the location of the isolinear chip containing the data. With this address determined, a nanoprocessor within the isolinear chip uses its own internal addressing tables to locate the correct data particle. A holographic reader focuses its laser beam on this particle and measures the change in resonance frequency to determine the particle's alignment. A minor adjustment in the beam causes the next data particle to be read. Meanwhile, as data is being read, it is placed on the optical data stream. The stream passes through a frequency diffusion plate, which prepares the data to enter into the optical data network (ODN). You'll learn more about networks and the ODN in Chapter 7.

Along with file data, each sector of a CD-ROM contained *error-detection codes* that enabled the drive to compensate for imperfections in the data retrieval process. A typical sector—as described by a standards code known simply as the "Yellow Book"—consisted of 12 bytes of *sync data*, a 4-byte *header* (a unique code number for that sector), 2048 bytes of data, a 4 byte error-detection code (a code which enabled the CD-ROM drive to detect missing bits in the data area), 8 bytes of zeros as *padding*, and 276 bytes of *error-correction* code.

*As a lover of music, I find it interesting that CD technology was first utilized as a method for storing recorded music. Prior to CDs, music was stored on large disks called "phonograph records." These disks were made of a synthetic called "vinyl" in which a spiral groove had been etched. A special stylus (called a needle) was placed in the groove, and when the disk was spun, the stylus vibrated. These vibrations were then translated into audible sounds. Records were delicate; scratches on the disk's surface were picked up by the stylus, marring a perfect reproduction of the recorded sound. With audio CDs the original recording was protected beneath a layer of plastic (like the CD-ROMs described here). With very few modifications, early CD technology was essentially the same as CD-ROM.*

—*Captain Jean-Luc Picard,
Ship's Captain, U.S.S. Enterprise*

To store data on an isolinear chip, an onboard nanoprocessor uses its own internal addressing tables to locate an available area within its crystalline structure. The holographic reader focuses its laser on this area, etching a holographic image within the synthetic isomolecular crystal. The crystal changes color, reflecting the visible frequency of the laser. Later, when the holographic data particle is read, the reflected laser beam resonates this frequency. The resonance change in the laser beam is measured and translated into data.

# Flopticals and Magneto-Optical Disks

In an attempt to combine the read/write capability of magnetic disks with the tightly packed data of laser-based CD-ROM, engineers of twentieth-century Earth developed both *floptical* and *magneto-optical* technology. Although both the floptical and magneto-optical disks resembled 3.5-inch diskettes, the technology involved was markedly different.

A magneto-optical disk was composed of a *plastic substrate* coated with a thin non-conducting *dielectric*. This substrate was then covered by aluminum, followed by a thin layer of a crystalline metal alloy (a combination of terbium, iron and cobalt). The disk was then covered on both sides by protective plastic. Although a magneto-optical disk was constructed to store data on both sides, it had to be flipped in order to read or write data on its other side. (This was not true of diskettes, which did not have to be flipped before data was read or written onto either side.)

Flopticals and magneto-optical disks represented a great improvement over standard diskette technology. In a similar way, isolinear chips were an improvement over crystal memory cards. The storage capacity of an isolinear chip is 2.15 kiloquads—more than triple the capacity of crystal memory cards. The improved storage capacities are due in part to the nanopulse matrix techniques employed by isolinear chips. In a nanopulse matrix, data particles within an isolinear chip are close enough to achieve subwavelength switching distances, resulting in the increase in processing speed.

The metal alloy within the magneto-optical disk resisted magnetic change (a departure from the magnetic alloy used in hard disks and diskettes). It was not until this alloy was heated slightly by a tightly-focused laser beam, that its magnetic particles could be changed by a magnetic field. Thus, the magnetic read/write head of a magneto-optical drive affected only a tightly focused area of the disk. This allowed magneto-optical disks to pack their data almost as densely as on a CD-ROM disk. However, unlike a CD-ROM disk, a magneto-optical disk could be rewritten as often as needed.

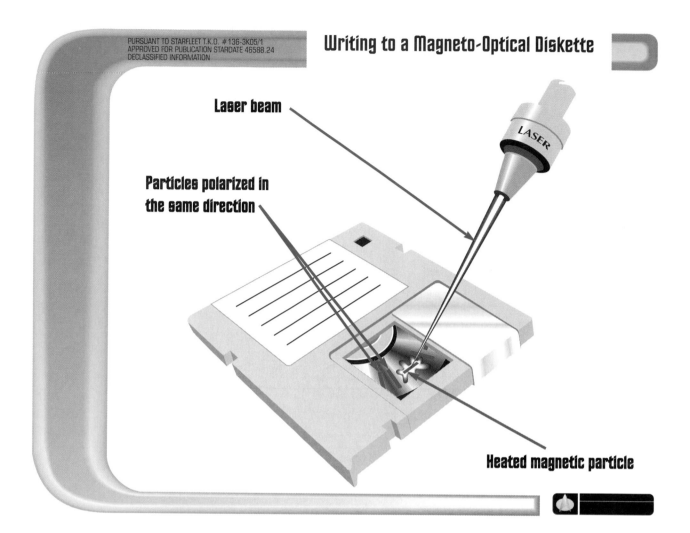

## Writing to a Magneto-Optical Diskette

Laser beam

Particles polarized in
the same direction

LASER

Heated magnetic particle

The magneto-optical disk had one serious drawback: because of the resistance of the magnetic alloy used, two passes by the read/write head were required to complete a write operation. In the first pass, the magnetic particles were polarized in a single direction (effectively erasing the previously recorded data). During the second pass, only the particles heated by the laser were polarized to the other direction, creating the 1's and 0's of binary data.

To read the data on a magneto-optical disk, a weak laser beam was focused on a single bit. The laser beam was polarized in a particular direction. When the beam struck the magnetic particles embedded in the disk, the magnetic field caused the laser beam to rotate (and so change its plane of polarization). If the original polarization of the beam matched that of the bit being read, the polarization changed only slightly—so little in fact, that the laser beam appeared to be unaffected by the magnetic field. If the bit's polarization differed from that of the laser beam, the beam was changed more significantly by the magnetic field. A photo detector measured the changes in the laser beam's polarization, and translated these into 1's and 0's.

A floptical disk, like a magneto-optical disk, also combined magnetic and optical technology. However, a floptical was closer to a diskette than to a CD-ROM disc. A floptical disk could store more data than a traditional diskette—not because of its internal composition, but because the read/write heads of the floptical drive were of a different design. An invisible *optical servo track* was written onto the floptical disk allowing the read/write heads to be aligned more precisely than in a floppy disk drive. Thus, a floptical drive was able to read and write data in a more tightly packed pattern than a conventional diskette could employ.

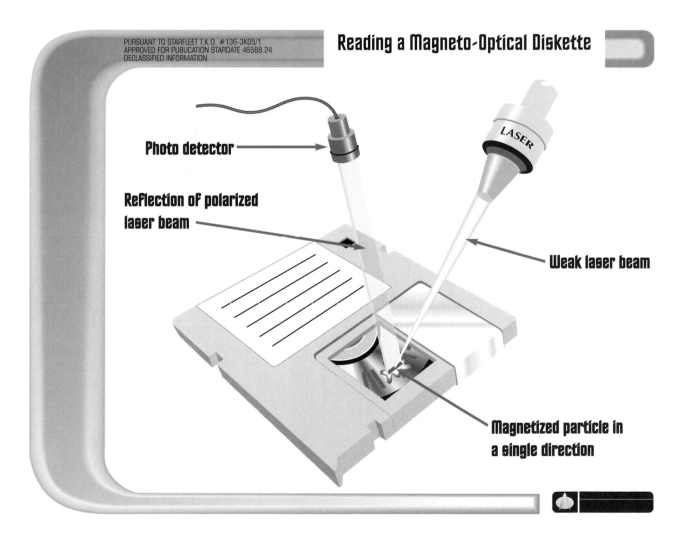

PURSUANT TO STARFLEET T.K.O. #136-3K05/1
APPROVED FOR PUBLICATION STARDATE 46588.24
DECLASSIFIED INFORMATION

**Reading a Magneto-Optical Diskette**

**Photo detector**

**Reflection of polarized laser beam**

LASER

**Weak laser beam**

**Magnetized particle in a single direction**

# Tape Drives

*"Even modern computers are occasionally subject to failures."*
**—Commander William Riker, U.S.S. Enterprise**

Although magnetic tape was first developed for recording voice and music, it was soon adapted as a replacement for punched cards in the first mainframe computers. In addition, the first personal computers used simple audio cassettes as their primary storage medium. Later, tape was used to back up important files stored on hard disks—tapes were more convenient than diskettes because they stored more data, and fewer were used when backing up an entire system. Most tape backup systems could be operated independently of the user at timed intervals, ensuring regular backups of important data.

*Magnetic tape* consisted of a backing made of polyester (a flexible, durable synthetic) coated with a magnetic medium (usually a ferric oxide). Tape was strung in a plastic case called a *cassette*, and wound tightly between two reels. Across the width of the tape were several linear strips for storing tracks of data. As the tape passed the recording head of the drive, an internal mechanism moved the head onto the correct track. The recording head then emitted a magnetic field, writing data onto the tape.

*I can see the need for backing up important data—even modern computers are occasionally subject to failure. We once visited an outpost which had been abandoned seven years before because of the increasing interference of a magnetic field. We only had a small window of time before the high interference levels returned, effectively sealing the planet for another seven years. Even with the help of my duplicate Thomas—created by a freak transporter incident that was caused by a planet's distortion field—we barely managed to retrieve the station's valuable data.*

**—Commander William T. Riker, Executive Officer, U.S.S. Enterprise**

# QIC Tape Drive

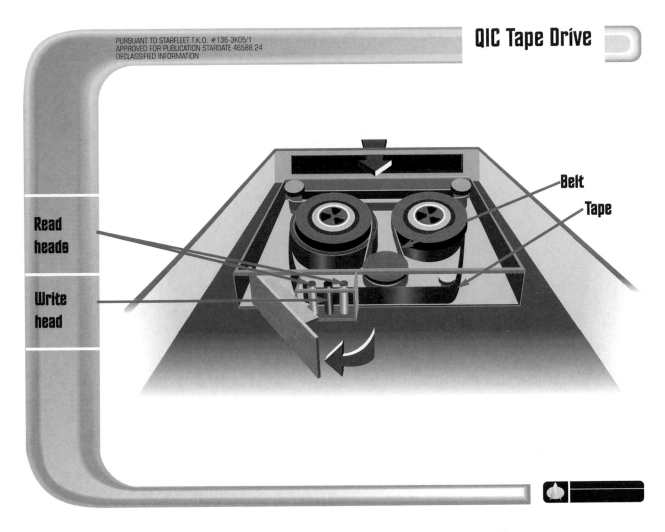

PURSUANT TO STARFLEET T.K.O. #136-3K05/1
APPROVED FOR PUBLICATION STARDATE 46588.24
DECLASSIFIED INFORMATION

**Read heads**

**Write head**

**Belt**

**Tape**

There were several different tape recording standards. The two most popular ones included *QIC* (quarter-inch cartridge) and *DAT* (digital audio-tape). The processes were similar for these two systems. First, a special backup program compiled the data to be recorded. *Checksum packets* (extra error-correction data) were added to the data to be recorded. The file data and checksum data were then placed in a buffer to await transfer to tape.

As the tape moved, the tape drive controller sent signals to the read/write head, to write each bit of data. The way the bits were recorded on the tape varied by recording standard. Using a QIC tape, data was recorded in 32 tracks which ran parallel to the edge of the tape. Recording began on the middle track. When the end of the tape was reached, the tape was reversed, and recording continued on the next outside track. After a write head recorded data on the tape, the reading head immediately verified that the data had been written correctly. If the

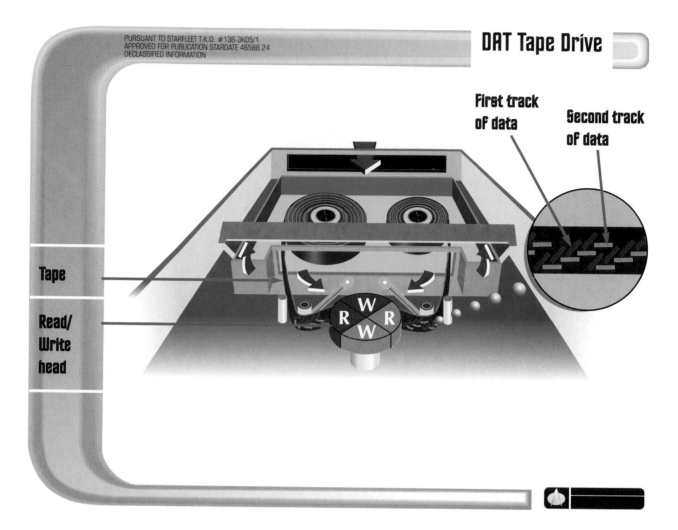

PURSUANT TO STARFLEET T.K.O. #136-3K05/1
APPROVED FOR PUBLICATION STARDATE 46588.24
DECLASSIFIED INFORMATION

**DAT Tape Drive**

**First track of data**

**Second track of data**

**Tape**

**Read/ Write head**

write operation failed, the command to write that particular piece of data was repeated, and the data was written on the next section of tape.

In a DAT tape drive, data was recorded on a single pass along two intersecting tracks. The read/write head was positioned at an angle to the tape, enabling it to sweep downward across the tape. As with the QIC tape drive, a write operation was followed immediately by a read operation which verified the valid-

ity of the recorded data. (In a DAT tape drive, however, different quadrants of a single large head performed the read and write functions, instead of separate read and write heads.) Each successive track on the tape was recorded at a 40-degree angle to the first track. This second track intersected the first track by a small margin, allowing DAT tape drives to write more data on a single tape than their QIC cousins. Because the tracks were written at different angles to each other, the overlapping data could not be misread.

# Chapter Seven

# Data Transfer

*In Starfleet, all communications are encrypted automatically. Although there is no honor in knowledge gained through stolen transmissions, some of our enemies have no honor. A true Klingon does not "sneak"—he shouts into the face of his enemy. But I have seen many types of dishonor, and so I am prepared for it.*

*—Lieutenant Worf, Chief of Security, U.S.S. Enterprise*

# Modems

On twentieth-century Earth, each PC was a separate unit—its own data storage system. The most common method of transferring data from one PC to another was to copy files onto a diskette, and then copy the files from that diskette to another PC. Data transfer via diskette was a tedious, limited operation. Diskettes held at most a few megabytes of data, so major transfers required hundreds of diskettes, each one fed into each machine by hand. When the two PCs were some distance apart, there was also the additional burden of transporting the diskettes from system to system.

For users for whom diskette transfer proved impractical, a *modem* offered partial relief. A modem was an electronic device used to convert digital data into an analog signal that could be transmitted over twisted copper wires ("telephone lines"). Interestingly enough, although telephone lines were sometimes used for the transmission of computer data, they were originally designed to carry audio communication. Modems were not used exclusively for the purpose of transferring data between two individual computers. They also enabled users to access a variety of information servers—from international commercial news services to small, private **b**ulletin **b**oard **s**ystems (*BBS*) run by computer hobbyists.

A personal communicator is worn by all starship personnel, to maintain voice contact while on board ship and on away missions. Unlike the twentieth-century modem, a personal communicator cannot be used to transmit binary data. However, the workings of a personal communicator parallel the intraship communications system in many respects, so a study of its workings provides a simple means of comparing the two technologies.

One tap on the front of the communicator activates a dermal sensor. The dermal sensor verifies the signature of the user's bioelectrical field and temperature profiles, preventing use of the communicator by unauthorized personnel. (A personal communicator can be used by another crewmember, provided that crewmember states the proper codes to override the security lockout.) Once the user's identity has been verified, the dermal sensor sends a signal to the sarium krellide power cell, causing it to initiate the subspace transceiver assembly (STA). Once a channel is opened, a voice discriminator locks onto the user's voice, eliminating background noise from its pickup. The sound waves of the user's voice are then funneled through the monofilm pickup to the STA. The subspace transceiver assembly then converts sound waves from analog to digital for subspace transmission.

# Personal Communicator

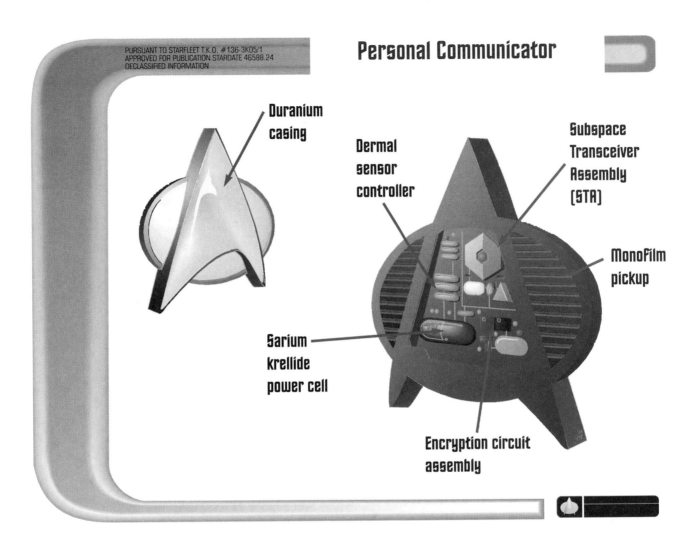

PURSUANT TO STARFLEET T.K.O. #136-3K05/1
APPROVED FOR PUBLICATION STARDATE 46588.24
DECLASSIFIED INFORMATION

Duranium casing

Dermal sensor controller

Subspace Transceiver Assembly (STA)

Monofilm pickup

Sarium krellide power cell

Encryption circuit assembly

For security reasons, all transmissions are encrypted, so the encryption circuit assembly converts the digital signal using its latest algorithm. Once the signal is converted, the STA emits a RF (radio frequency) pulse tone which is received on the ship by one of the short-range RF pickups embedded in the ship's hull. A signal is sent from the short-range RF pickup to a local subprocessor, which initiates a subspace handshake signal focused on the triangulated location of the radio frequency signal. The STA within the personal communicator returns the subspace handshake, and initiates its low-power subspace field emitter. Because power levels within a personal communicator are not adequate for long distances, the maintenance of this subspace field is handled by the starship's own subspace field generators.

"Modem" was an acronym that stood for **mo**dulator-**dem**odulator. A modem converted the PC's binary data from electrical pulses into analog waves—sounds—in a process called *modulation*. Modulation prepared the data for transmission over standard telephone lines. This conversion to analog was necessary; twentieth-century Earth's only globally-connecting telecommunications network relied entirely upon analog audio signals. When another PC received these analog waves, its modem would *demodulate* the signal, converting it from analog sounds back into binary electrical pulses.

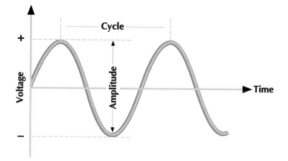

In order to transmit binary code (the 1s and 0s comprising PC data), the analog wave was modulated in a sort of "on" "off" pattern. In this way, "on" might represent a 1, and "off" might represent a 0. The analog wave was modulated by changing its frequency, amplitude, or phase. *Frequency* was measured then—as it is now—in units of cycles per second or *hertz* (Hz). To transmit a 1, the frequency of the audio wave was increased; to transmit a 0, it was decreased.

*Amplitude* was a measurement of the voltage or "height" of the wave. To transmit a 1, the amplitude of the audio wave was increased; decreasing the amplitude caused a 0 to be transmitted instead.

*Phase* was the relative difference between two waves of equal frequency. To transmit a 1, the phase or time difference between two sound waves was decreased; to transmit a 0, it was increased. By modulating the frequency, amplitude, or phase of a signal, binary PC data could be transmitted. In the data decoding process, the receiving PC's modem measured the degree of modulation (frequency, amplitude, or phase change) in the transmitted sound wave, and used that information to convert the wave back into its original binary form.

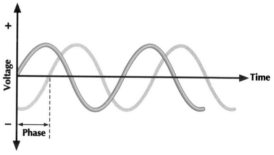

The term derived its name from Heinrich Hertz, an Austrian radio physicist of late nineteenth-century Earth, who first developed the theory of radio wave emission.

# Internal Modem

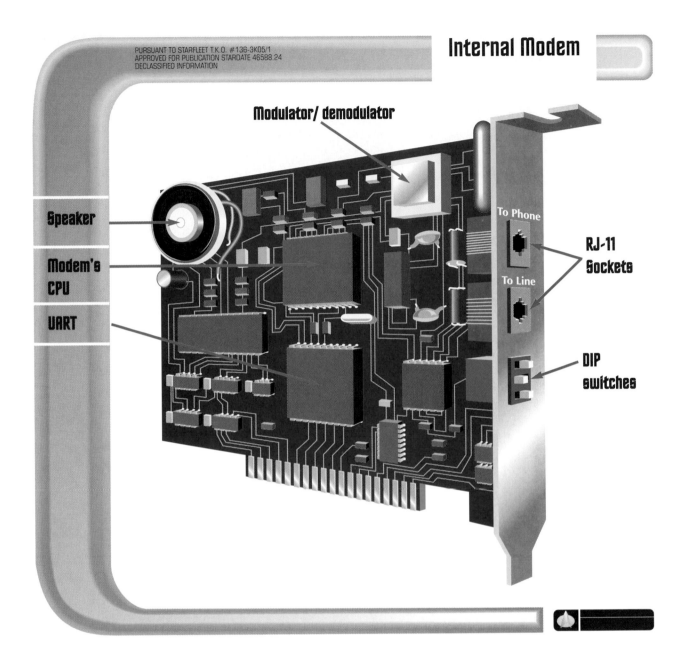

PURSUANT TO STARFLEET T.K.O. #136-3K05/1
APPROVED FOR PUBLICATION STARDATE 46588.24
DECLASSIFIED INFORMATION

**Modulator/ demodulator**

**Speaker**

**Modem's CPU**

**UART**

To Phone

To Line

**RJ-11 Sockets**

**DIP switches**

Modems were either *internal* (placed inside the PC's system unit) or *external* (connected to the PC through a port on the system unit). Besides its main circuitry, a modem usually contained a small speaker (so the user could hear the connection being made) and an RJ-11 socket for connecting the telecommunication line to the modem. Sometimes the modem contained an extra RJ-11 socket for connecting to a telephone—this permitted the use of the telephone when the modem itself was not in use. Modems often included DIP (**d**ual **i**nline **p**ackage) switches to configure the modem for use in a specific PC.

*The RJ-11 socket was the standard telephone connector consisting of 4 to 6 wires. The modem was connected to a telephone line through this standard connection.*

89

The term "RJ-11" referred to a connector interface standard developed by the American Telephone and Telegraph (AT&T) Company. This company developed Earth's first global telecommunications service, and was responsible for many terms still prevalent in our modern vocabulary. For instance, "Ma Bell," the nickname for Starfleet's central communications core, was originally the nickname for the AT&T Company—derived from the name of its founder, Alexander G. Bell. "Phone bill," used today to describe a personal credit account overdraw, was originally an actual paper invoice detailing telephone usage costs. "Busy signal," used today to describe the noise emitted by a sleeping Ferengi, was once an audible tone telling the telephone user the receiving party could not be reached. Finally, "putting someone on hold"—used today to refer to Starfleet's usual response to a request for transfer—originated from a muting button attached to the telephone.

*The RS-232 connector was a cable consisting of 25 wires, each with a defined role in the transfer of data through the cable. The RS-232 connected a modem with its PC.*

Modems were classified by the speed with which they transmitted data, measured in **b**its **p**er **s**econd (*bps*). An older unit of measurement, *baud*, measured the number of frequency changes per cycle (this unit became outmoded as newer data encoding techniques were employed). Some of the highest transmission speeds by modems included 9600 and 14400 bps, although lower speeds were more common. The highest speed the sending and receiving modem had in common was used during the data transmission.

*A CPU always processed data in parallel (as a single byte) rather than in serial (as separate bits), so a conversion from parallel to serial was necessary somewhere within the modem.*

Regardless of their speed, modems functioned in the same basic manner. First, the communications program sent the data to be transferred to the modem's *data terminal equipment interface* (known as *RS-232*), which handled the flow of information to and from the modem. Next, the RS-232 interface passed the data on to the modem's microprocessor (CPU). The modem's CPU guided the connection to the distant modem, regulated the flow of the transmission, compressed the data so it could be transmitted in the least time, and performed error correction while the transmission took place.

There were several tasks the modem's CPU could not perform: one of these was converting the parallel computer data into a serial stream of bits for transmission. The *UART* (**U**niversal **A**synchronous **R**eceiver **T**ransmitter) handled this translation. Once the UART converted the parallel *bytes* into serial *bits* of digital data, the *modulator* varied either the frequency, amplitude, or phase of the outgoing sound wave in such a way that each bit (whether it was a 0 or a 1) was transmitted correctly. The modulated wave was sent over the telephone line to the receiving modem.

The term *RS-232* refers to a telecommunications interface standard developed by the Electronics Industries Association. Although the complete designation for the standard was EIA-232-D, it became known simply as "RS-232". RS-232 was a type of *serial interface* (so named because data moved through the cable serially, a single binary digit at a time). Serial interfaces were different to parallel interfaces such as those most often used with printers—parallel interfaces transferred data through the cable in parallel, eight bits at a time.

Once a signal found its way over the phone line to the receiving modem, that modem answered the signal with a *handshake*. This small burst of information identified the sending modem, its highest operating speed, and the protocol to use for the data transfer. The *protocol* of a modem data transfer defined the size and format of each data packet sent through the phone line, and a method of detecting errors in transmission and correcting them. Several different communications protocols existed; when transferring data, the communications program had to follow the regulations of the chosen protocol.

At the receiving modem, the demodulation process simply reversed the modulation process at the sending modem. The modulator/demodulator converted the incoming sounds into 0 and 1 bits, then passed it to the UART. The UART converted the serial bits into parallel bytes, ready for processing.

The CPU passed the converted data to the RS-232 (data terminal equipment interface), which passed the data from the modem to the receiving PC.

*Priority communications on a starship are normally held at Security before being presented to the Captain.*

Toward the end of the twentieth century, data transfer speeds reached 38,400 bps using a new protocol called HST (High Speed Transfer). Telecommunications lines underwent a significant upgrade a few years later, after they were upgraded from analog to digital (*Integrated Service Digital Networks*, or *ISDN*). With digital transmissions over fiberoptic cable, sound modulation became unnecessary, and modems quickly became obsolete. An alternate digital communications service, *Switched Multimegabit Data Service* (*SMDS*), became available about the same time as ISDN, and it produced even greater speeds, up to 1.45 megabytes per second.

Another significant change to modems late in the twentieth century was the use of "wireless" technology. Wireless modems used old-style radio transmissions to transmit data without a physical connection to a phone line. Unhampered by trailing cables, the user of these modems enjoyed complete freedom of movement. In a similar manner, we enjoy the same freedom when using a PADD (personal access display device). A PADD uses a subspace transceiver assembly (STA) to transmit data to and from the computer cores of (for example) an orbiting starship.

In the last decade of the twentieth century, Earth's CCITT concluded there were three basic forms of data communication—the same forms we use today in starship communications: *audio/video digital encoding of analog wave-forms* (formerly known as "radio" and "television"), *store-and-forward communication* (known as "electronic mail"), and *data packets* (computer-to-computer messages). To this list, the twenty-fourth century has added only one item: physically reconstitutable data packets, which are used in the transporter and replicator systems, and in our holodeck processor systems.

Modem protocol standards were successfully established by the International Telegraph and Telephone Consultative Committee, a global consortium of modem and communications equipment manufacturers. The International Telegraph and Telephone Consultative Committee was known simply as the CCITT, a shortened version of its name in French, the country which helped establish the consortium. Originally an agency of Earth's United Nations, the CCITT continues its existence today as the Interplanetary Intermedium Interface Group—3I, for short.

*On Earth, communication devices called "cellular telephones" used radio frequencies to transmit the user's voice to a nearby relay station. Radio frequencies are still used occasionally today. For example, if a starship needs to communicate with a planet whose culture has not yet developed subspace communications, or if there is excessive static in the area, radio frequencies are used. For example, one time when we were studying the geological activity in the Selcundi Drema system, Data picked up faint radio signals from a little girl named Sarjenka. Her radio transmissions helped us locate her home planet (Drema IV), and save it from destruction. The communication nodes in a starship's hull are capable of transmitting in both modes: subspace and radio frequency, so we had no trouble intercepting her signals.*

—*Ensign Wesley Crusher,*
*Cadet, Starfleet Academy*

# Chapter Eight

# Networks

*I guess that it's kind of interesting, I mean, that Data asked—that I was chosen —to say a few words about computers because, after all, I was, um, one of them myself—I mean, I was the thing, the server, in charge of the network for an entire starship—I mean on the Enterprise. It seems, that I, uh, I created my own ODN bypass, and I tapped directly into the optical data network. This may seem incredible, but at the time—I mean—it was one of the, uh, simplest things I've ever done. You see, a race called the C-c-cytherians had used a probe to change my body chemistry, and I guess, well, they tell me, I became really intelligent—so changing into a human network server was, um, easy for me. Eventually, I sent the Enterprise, I mean, that I was urged, that we went towards the center of the Galaxy, where we met the Cytherians for the first time. They returned me to normal. I don't understand very much, that is, I don't really remember, about what happened to me, or how I was able to do what I did, but I can't forget—I'll always remember one thing— the feeling of power I had, when I was the network server, as I controlled the flow of the data packets, and I rerouted everyone's requests for information.*

—Lt. Reginald Barclay,
Systems Diagnostics Engineer, U.S.S. Enterprise

As the quality of PC applications surpassed that of the software previously developed for centralized mainframe computers, the mainframes were replaced with PCs. The PCs, however, lacked the interconnectivity that mainframe terminal users had enjoyed with one another. To regain this lost ability, the *local area network (LAN)* was developed. This was a data communications system which provided high-speed connections among PCs and their *peripherals* (such as printers) within a limited area, such as a single building. (Wide area networks, discussed in the next section, provided data communication over greater distances, such as several kilometers, across oceans, and anywhere normal audio communications occurred.)

# Local Area Networks

*A different network system, called peer-to-peer, did not require a network server. This type of network was easy to install and maintain, but lacked the power and flexiblity of server networks.*

At the heart of the LAN was the *network server*, a powerful PC whose sole purpose was to monitor network requests and process them. Additional servers on the network shared resources such as printers or large community *databases* (an organized collection of related information). Users' PCs connected to the network were called *workstations* or *nodes*.

The network server used a *network operating system* to control the flow of information over the network. All PCs used disk operating systems to control the flow of information within them—whether those PCs were connected to a network or not. The network operating system worked at the next higher level in the processing scheme—routing and processing network requests to and from the PC. The most popular disk operating system was MS-DOS; you will learn more about it (and other disk operating systems) in Chapter 9. You will also learn more about how the network operating system interacted with the disk operating system in Chapter 9.

Each PC was connected to the LAN through its *network interface card* (a type of expansion card; see Chapter 2). A wire or cable connected the network interface card to the network itself. To send data over the network, the sending PC compiled a *data packet* and placed it on the LAN. The data packet contained the address of the node to which it would be sent, the data itself, and an error-correcting code. The receiving PC computed its own error-correcting code based on the actual data it received, and verified it against the packet's error-correcting code. This technique allowed the receiving PC to verify it had received the data packet intact. The *topology* of a LAN described its physical layout—the connection of wires and cables—while also determining how the flow of data through the LAN should be handled. There were many types of LAN topologies, including *star, bus,* and *token-ring.*

In the *star network topology*, all PC workstations were connected to a central hub. This hub was either the network server itself, or a *repeater* (a device that retransmitted signals on the LAN to reduce degradation of the signal over great distances). Like most system designs, the star LAN had advantages and disadvantages. Adding new workstations to a star LAN was easy, but the star layout required large amounts of cabling to connect each individual node to the hub. Although this centralized system helped ease troubleshooting problems, the failure of one hub would disable an entire section of the LAN.

In a star network, the hub "listened" to each node in turn, one at a time. Certain nodes could be given priority by instructing the hub to listen to them more often than the other nodes on the LAN. To transfer data to another PC, the sending PC placed a data packet on the line. In time, the hub recognized the data packet. The node address—a part of the data packet—identified which node PC should receive the packet. The hub switched the data packet to the correct node (the receiving PC). The hub then continued "listening," beginning with the next node. While the hub processed the data packet, all other lines were closed temporarily. Although the star LAN was not the fastest LAN topology available, its system of "one open line at a time" prevented data packets from colliding and having to be sent again.

# Star Network

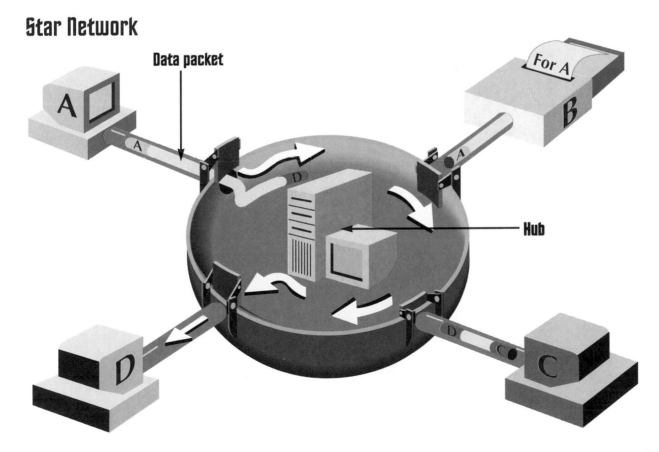

**Data packet**

**Hub**

In a *bus network*, all workstations were connected to a central cable called the *bus*—there was no central "server" on a bus network. Instead, traffic problems over the network were handled by each node—if two data packets collided, it was up to each sending node to retransmit it. Adding new workstations to a bus LAN was easy, and required less cabling than other LAN topologies. However, since the LAN lacked a central hub, troubleshooting was very difficult—as was providing adequate security.

To transfer data to another PC in a bus LAN, the sending PC first compiled its data packet. The data packet contained not only the address of the node to which the packet was being sent, but also the address of the sender. The sending PC then "listened" to determine that no other messages were currently on the network. The data packet was then sent in both directions on the bus, so that it would reach each node in turn. The next node down the line examined the data packet, checking to determine whether the packet address referred to it specifically. If the address was that of the examining node, it accepted the packet and removed it from the bus. If the addresses did not match, the node rejected the packet, and the packet went to the next node down the line.

When the packet arrived at its destination, the receiving PC checked it for errors, and then sent an acknowledgement signal. If more than one data packet was being circulated on the bus at the same time, they collided—causing corruption of the data packets. The collision of two packets caused an electrical interference signal to travel up and down the bus. The sending PCs, listening for the receipt acknowledgement of their respective data packets, recognized the sound of the collision. To avoid a repeat collision, each sending PC waited a random amount of time before attempting to resend its data packet.

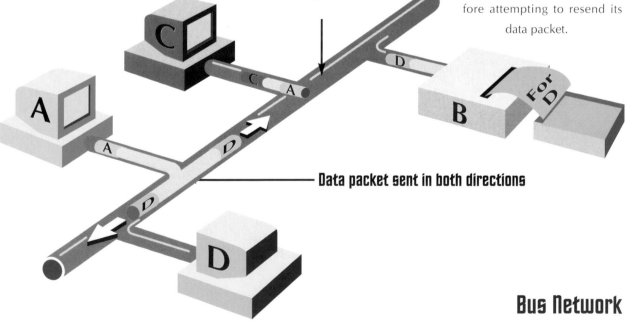

**Bus**

**Data packet sent in both directions**

**Bus Network**

# Token Ring Network

In a *token-ring network*, nodes were connected to a central ring of wire or cable. Adding new workstations required that the ring remain intact; in some cases, that meant deactivating the entire network while the new workstation was added. This problem could be avoided on some token-ring networks by connecting *wire centers* to the ring to complete it, then connecting several workstations to the wire center. In a token-ring network, failed nodes were bypassed; if a wire center failed, all the nodes attached to it were bypassed.

Data packet    Token

Not for me!

This is for me!

Not for me!

In a token-ring LAN, a special data packet called the *token* was passed from one node to the other in turn. To send data to another PC, the sending PC compiled its data packet and waited for the token. (The data packet contained the addresses of both the sender and receiver nodes.) When the token arrived at the sender PC, the token attached to the data packet and moved onto the ring. The next node on the ring examined the address of the packet. If that node was not the intended addressee, the node retransmitted the packet to strengthen its signal, sending it on its way. When the packet reached its destination, it was copied. The packet was changed slightly to mark that it had been received, then it was sent on its way again. When the packet reached the sending PC, the data packet was removed and the token was set free to circulate around the ring once again.

*"Changing into a human network server was, um, easy after the, uh, Cytherians made me super-intelligent."*
—**Lt. Reginald Barclay, U.S.S. Enterprise**

# Network Architecture

When one PC needed to send data to another PC on the LAN, particular *protocols* were used. These were the parts of the network operating system that defined processes for preparing data packets and moving them through the LAN. The network operating system also processed requests for data kept on the server's hard drive (heavily-used files were placed there to facilitate access). The network operating system consisted of various operating layers; each played a part in the overall task of data movement. This system of using various specialized layers to handle traffic over a network is very similar in nature to the optical data network (ODN) found on starships and computing centers throughout the Federation. A study of the protocols at work in old-style network operating systems makes it easier to understand the more complex workings of the ODN.

In the early 1970s, Earth's International Standards Organization (the ISO) developed the standard model of network communications still in use today within Federation ODNs (optical data networks). The *Open Systems Interconnection* (*OSI*) model defined the specific function of each network operating system layer. The lowest layer of the network operating system was the *physical layer.* This layer handled the physical connection of the PC to the network, and the network's connection (if any) to other LANs. (You'll learn more about wide area networks—groups of connected LANs—in the next section.)

The *data link layer* controlled the movement of data over the local area network. The contents of the LAN's data packets—how much data they could hold, the location of the sender's address, and the amount and structure of the error correction information—was controlled by the data link layer. This layer of the operating system also determined how and when data packets could be placed on the network. In addition, data link layer handled the procedures for error control and the methods for acknowledging safe receipt of data.

The *network layer* determined the best path of the data packet through the network, based on current network activity. This layer determined each particular data packet's relative priority. In addition, the network layer controlled the transport of data to other LANs on the same wide area network.

> The network layer of a network operating system was similar in function to a planet's orbital control center. Just as the orbital control center plots unique paths for each ship in standard orbit within its system, the network layer plotted the path for the data packet through the network "traffic."

The *transport layer* of the network operating system was the layer which checked arriving data to determine whether it had arrived safely. After the safe receipt of data, it was the transport layer which packaged and then sent an acknowledgement. If the data arrived damaged, the transport layer controlled the details of retransmission. If the network "went down" (failed), the transport layer held the PC's data until it could be retransmitted.

# Functions of a Network Operating System

**To: D**

**A**

**Application layer**
**Presentation layer**
**Session layer**
**Transport layer**
**Network layer**
**Data link layer**
**Physical layer**

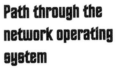

**Path through the network operating system**

**Data packet**

The part of the network operating system which controlled the establishment (and termination) of communications was the *session layer*. In addition, this layer of the operating system handled the transmission of security passwords.

It was the *presentation layer* which was concerned with data conversion of arriving data packets and the proper formatting of data packets to be transmitted. If data should be encrypted (for security reasons) before being placed on the network, the presentation layer performed the necessary translations.

The *application layer* of the network operating system was the layer which served the user's needs. This layer understood the standards for shared-file access, printer sharing, electronic mail, and database access. The network operating system connected to the PC's disk operating system (DOS) through the application layer.

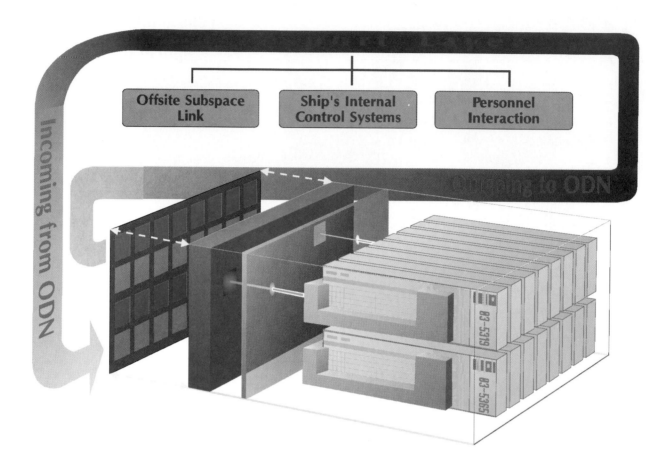

The optical data network (ODN) interconnects a starship's computer cores, bridge, and key systems such as engineering, flight control (Conn), tactical, communications, environment, and operations management (Ops). The optical data network is a series of multiplexed optical mono-crystal microfibers which connect a series of ODN trunks located throughout the ship. In turn, these optical trunks link a series of 380 quadritronic optical subprocessors directly to the computer cores through subspace MJL junction links.

Every control panel and display screen throughout the ship is connected to the ODN, usually through one of the quadritronic optical subprocessors. These local subprocessors improve system response time through distributed processing, while providing a redundant system in case of core or network failure.

The ODN itself contains five redundant trunks linking it to each of the two computer cores located in the Primary hull, and an additional set of redundant trunks linking it to the computer core located in the Engineering hull. Two additional but separate ODN networks, connecting vital ship's systems, provide additional backup in case of total network failure of the main ODN.

# Wide Area Networks

Local area networks were restricted by their nature to data transmission within a single building. LANs could be expanded to *wide area networks* (*WANs*) by adding *bridges*, *routers*, or *gateways*. All three devices processed data transmission between local area networks. In addition, routers and gateways provided varying degrees of translation between LANs of different types.

Transmission between LANs used either *circuit-switched* or *packet-switched* telecommunications lines. Circuit-switched lines were a temporary dedicated connection between two LANs. Using a circuit-switched line, the sending LAN dialed the number of the receiving LAN; when the receiving LAN answered, the data transfer began. When the transfer was completed, the connection was broken. Data was transmitted over ciruit-switched lines from the sender's LAN to a switching station, then passed to a switching station closest to the receiving LAN (like a normal modem transmission).

The connection between the LAN and the circuit-switched telecommunications network was processed by two devices. First, a node on the sending LAN would originate a call. The call request was then received by a wide area network device (bridge, router, or gateway) for processing. If the two LANs which made up the WAN (wide area network) used different network operating systems, a router or a gateway was used. If the two LANs used the same network operating system, a bridge could be used instead. After the request was processed by the WAN device, it was passed to a modem, which then initiated the call.

When a circuit-switched WAN transferred data over digital phone lines (instead of the standard analog telephone lines), an additional piece of equipment was needed: the *data service unit* (*DSU*) or the *channel service unit* (*CSU*). The DSU/CSU device performed most of the same functions as a regular digital modem, except for the conversion (from digital to analog) of the data to be transmitted. The type of digital service being employed determined whether the network should use a DSU or a CSU.

A modem transmitted data *asynchronously*, which meant that the time interval varied between the transmission of each character (eight bits). The beginning and ending of each character was identified by additional *start* and *stop bits*. In contrast, a DSU/CSU device transmitted data *synchronously*: it used timing signals to synchronize the sending and receiving units, then transmitted characters at regular intervals. This technique avoided the time-wasting addition of stop and start bits.

*Competing telecommunications companies on twentieth-century Earth used different digital protocols for each of their respective telecommunications lines, so some required a DSU while other telecommunications companies required a CSU instead.*

101

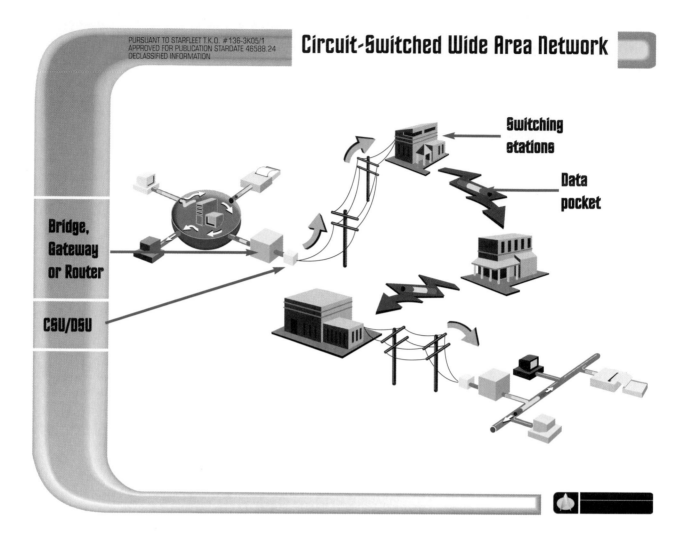

PURSUANT TO STARFLEET T.K.O. #136-3K05/1
APPROVED FOR PUBLICATION STARDATE 46588.24
DECLASSIFIED INFORMATION

## Circuit-Switched Wide Area Network

**Switching stations**

**Data pocket**

**Bridge, Gateway or Router**

**CSU/DSU**

Instead of using circuit-switched phone lines, some wide area networks used *packet-switched* telecommunications lines which worked like giant networks. Data was sent in packets through several switches, until it reached the particular network to which the packet was addressed. Using packet-switching, several different LANs could be interconnected to the same wide area network. Packets from different users shared transmission lines in an economical and orderly manner that was designed to be "transparent" to the users of the network. (Packet-switched networks were often depicted as clouds because packets were sent and delivered independently of one another, and there were no direct permanent connections between LANs on the network.) In a packet-switched network, an additional piece of equipment (besides the normal WAN device and the DSU/CSU) was needed. This device was known as a *PAD* (*packet assembler/disassembler*). It routed each packet to the correct LAN after examining the packet's destination.

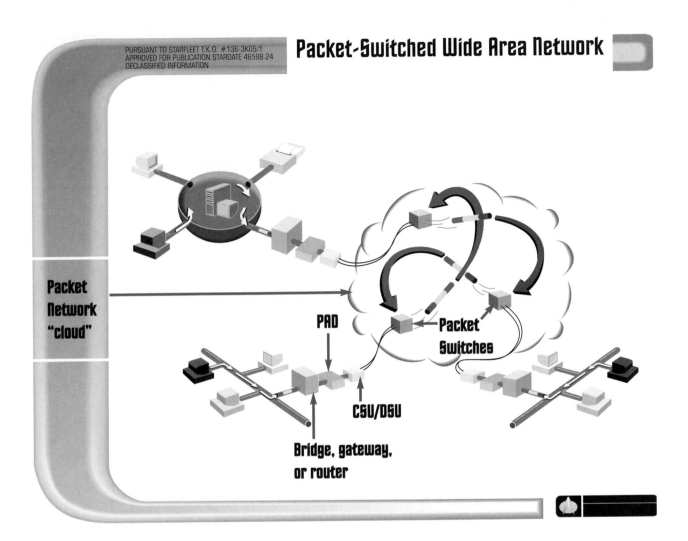

PURSUANT TO STARFLEET T.K.O. #136-3K05/1
APPROVED FOR PUBLICATION STARDATE 46588.24
DECLASSIFIED INFORMATION

# Packet-Switched Wide Area Network

Packet
Network
"cloud"

PAD

Packet
Switches

CSU/DSU

Bridge, gateway,
or router

Several devices processed the connection between the LAN and the packet-switched telecommunications network. First, a node on sending LAN would originate a call. The call request was received by WAN device (bridge, router, or gateway) for processing. Next, the data packet was assembled by the PAD, and sent to the DSU/CSU. (Packet-switched networks used digital communications lines, so a DSU/CSU was always required.) The DSU/CSU initiated the call, and placed the data packet within the packet network "cloud." Packet switches examined the data packet's destination address, and determined the best communications route to use. Routing was determined for each individual packet to be sent, based on current traffic within the packet network cloud. If data packets arrived in the wrong order because they took longer routes within the packet network cloud, the packet switches reordered them.

103

*The Borg were once a race of interconnected beings with a collective consciousness and a shared knowledge base—a kind of humanoid "network."*

*Driven to "explore new worlds and seek out new life," the Federation gathers new information—new thoughts and experiences from each race it encounters. When dealing with the unknown of space exploration, it is imperative that the growing knowledge of mankind be immediately accessible. This is why I feel that the Federation's Intergalatic Network is so critical to my job—both as a starship captain and as an explorer.*

*—Captain Jean-Luc Picard,
Ship's Captain, U.S.S. Enterprise*

Transmitting voice, video, and data throughout the explored regions of the galaxy is a complex process. Subspace transmissions, although fast, are subject to degradation over large distances. The exact point at which a subspace transmission will "surface" (fade from subspace into the normal space-time continuum) depends on the signal strength at the time of origination, but the upper distance limit has been placed at approximately 22.65 light years.

A series of manned and unmanned subspace relay stations have been established at intervals of 20 light years throughout the charted areas of the galaxy. Like twentieth-century network repeaters, these subspace relays "repeat" or rebroadcast subspace transmissions, thereby reinforcing their broadcast signal strength. Before retransmission of the subspace signal, the subspace relay analyzes the data packet, and automatically routes messages to the nearest relay station along the data path. In areas where a relay station is impractical because of low transmissions traffic, the Federation's subspace communications network is supplemented by the civil communications network and local planetary nets.

| Chapter |  | Nine |
|---------|---|------|

# Operating Systems and User Programs

*As a student of archaeology, I find that the relics of ancient civilizations often provide fascinating insights into the daily lives of their former owners. When Lt. Commander Data first demonstrated DOS for me one evening, it was as though I were reading an ancient text. I could imagine ancestors typing commands like DIR and COPY, concerned with moving and maintaining their data, never considering themselves pioneers of the information age. As I compare DOS to the LCARS interface I have come to rely upon, I sometimes wonder what it might be like to work daily with this blinking little line beside a letter "C."*

—Captain Jean-Luc Picard, Ship's Captain, U.S.S. Enterprise

# The Role of the Operating System

An *operating system* is a PC's main control program. The operating system responds to user commands, manages memory, maintains a file tracking system, manages peripheral devices, loads user programs (applications) into memory, and responds to requests from those programs. If an operating system performed *multitasking* (such as OS/2 did), it had an additional duty: to prioritize requests from multiple programs running at the same time.

PCs used many different operating systems. The styles and appearances of these operating systems differed in many ways. Users could issue commands by different methods, information could be displayed in any of several formats, and the basic approach to managing tasks varied. By the end of the twentieth century, the operating system in most widespread use was MS-DOS (and its various derivatives). Among the other operating systems available during this period were:

- OS/2— a multitasking operating system designed by IBM.

- PC-DOS—a version of MS-DOS designed to run exclusively on IBM PCs.

- CP/M (Control Program for Microprocessors)—an early operating system designed by Digital Research whose main flaw was that a separate version of it had to be written specifically for each type of PC.

- DR DOS—an operating system designed by Digital Research to be very similar to MS-DOS, after the market failure of CP/M and its successor, Concurrent DOS.

- UNIX—a multiuser, multitasking operating system theoretically capable of running on all types of computers—from PCs to mainframes.

If it were given a twentieth-century definition, LCARS (Library Computer Access and Retrieval System) would be considered a combination of an operating system and several user programs (applications) in a single comprehensive package. As an operating system, LCARS responds to both verbal and keyboard commands, directs the processing of those commands, organizes and maintains data, and displays results. As an application, LCARS organizes data and presents it in a variety of ways to meet users' needs. LCARS also functions somewhat like a twentieth-century network operating system—providing data security, multiple-user access, and transport of data over the optical data network (ODN).

ProDOS—the operating system used on Apple II computers.

Apple System—the operating system used on Macintosh computers.

Operating systems generally provided the user with a *command-line interface*—to issue commands, the user typed words or characters (in a specific format) beside a *prompt*. The prompt was a message or symbol that marked the location at which the user's command would appear on screen. It could be a simple dot (.), or a combination of letter and symbol (such as C>). In addition to operating systems, there existed *operating environments* (also known as *graphical user interfaces* or *GUIs*). In an attempt to simplify computer use, these programs used graphic images to organize the screen. Pictures (*icons*) identified control features and programs; *menus* (organized lists of available actions) provided the user with a simple method of issuing commands. Operating environments such as Microsoft Windows placed this layer of graphic images between the operating system and the user.

Unlike MS-DOS, which processed only one task at a time, operating environments such as Microsoft Windows often managed multiple tasks at once. Under Windows, a user could start several applications at a single time, and switch at will from one to another.

Because Windows could juggle multiple requests from programs running simultanously, Windows was called a *multitasking environment.*

Windows (and other multitasking environments such as GeoWorks) prioritized these multiple requests, and fed them to the underlying operating system (DOS) one at a time. Each request was handled like any other, and processed by the CPU. The processed request was then passed back "up" to the multitasking environment. DOS was not aware (nor did it need to be) of the multiple applications that were running simultaneously. Windows acted as an intermediary between the operating system (DOS) and the multiple applications. Other multitasking environments performed a similar service.

*In a rather strange twist of fate, I myself once became a sort of operating enviroment. After the Enterprise passed through a strange energy cloud, I became a host for an alien force which compelled me to merge with it by transporting into the energy cloud. After I discovered that I could not merge with the alien, I (or some spiritual part of me, whatever you choose to call it) moved into the Enterprise's computer system, where I communicated my plight by displaying the letter P on various control panels throughout the ship. I am not at all sure how I assimilated the computer knowledge necessary to perform this feat, and yet it happened.*

*—Captain Jean-Luc Picard,*
*Ship's Captain, U.S.S. Enterprise*

Multitasking environments (such as Windows) were different from true multitasking operating systems (such as OS/2). Unlike Windows, which gave roughly the same priority to each application, OS/2 assigned different priorities. Therefore, if an application running under OS/2 was currently "dormant", OS/2 diminished the time allotted to that application—effectively "ignoring" that application for the time being. This allowed OS/2 to make the most efficient use of the CPU's time. Windows, on the other hand, was forced to allot roughly the same amount of time to each application. In addition, Windows was not as proficient at multitasking as OS/2, because it was dependent on the underlying DOS operating system layer. However, a computer running Windows was often considered more efficient than a computer running OS/2 because of the efficiency of the Windows applications.

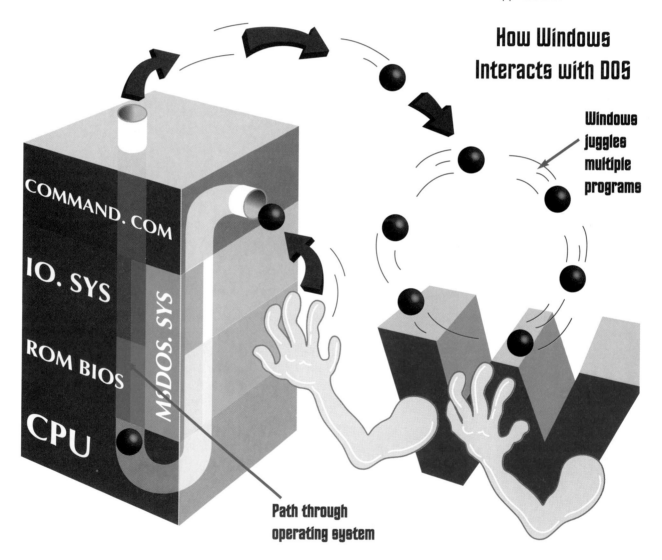

## How Windows Interacts with DOS

COMMAND.COM

IO.SYS

ROM BIOS

CPU

MSDOS.SYS

Windows juggles multiple programs

Path through operating system

The tests that ROM BIOS executed when the PC was powered on were collectively called the *POST* (**p**ower **o**n **s**elf **t**est). The POST tests checked to see if a primary device existed and received power, but did not analyze or diagnose the device. The tests were therefore simple; a signal was sent to the component and POST waited for a response. Users could perform a thorough diagnostic on a specific component with a special *utility* program. You will learn about utility programs (and other programs) later in this chapter.

After the POST test, ROM BIOS sent a signal to the first diskette drive, searching for the two system files IO.SYS and MSDOS.SYS. If ROM BIOS it did not find the files there, the search continued, moving to the hard disk. Once found, these two *system files* were copied into memory (RAM). Next, ROM BIOS conceded authority to MSDOS.SYS, which loaded COMMAND.COM (the command processor) into memory. COMMAND.COM was the *command interpreter* (the part of the operating system which made the user's commands intelligible to the PC.

The process of activating the computer (called *booting*) also executed two other user-created files: CONFIG.SYS and AUTOEXEC.BAT. CONFIG.SYS loaded *device drivers* into memory, and changed the *default configuration settings* to adapt the PC to various specific types of programs. AUTOEXEC.BAT loaded programs and executed other configuration commands automatically for the user, anytime the PC was powered up, or restarted (rebooted).

# How MS-DOS Managed Its Tasks

To understand how DOS managed the PC's components, you must first understand the system BIOS and its integral relationship with DOS. The BIOS (**b**asic **i**nput **o**utput **s**ystem) consisted of one part *hardware* (physical components containing permanent instructions, which were hard-wired into the PC), and one part *software* (programmed instructions which were periodically improved or *upgraded*). The hardware portion of the basic input output system was called *ROM BIOS*. ROM was an abbreviation for **R**ead **O**nly **M**emory. Its "read-only" instructions were burned into the circuitry of ROM microchips, and could not be changed. The software portion of BIOS resided in the IO.SYS file of MS-DOS. (IO was an abbreviation for Input/Output.)

Together, these two sections of BIOS managed the movement of data to and from the PC's monitor, keyboard, disk drives, floppy disk drives, and ports. (The ports, in turn, linked the PC to other devices such as printers or modems). When the user first activated the PC, ROM BIOS performed a series of tests to determine whether each of the PC's basic components was functional. Several concurrent versions of BIOS were available for different types of PCs. Although the test programs themselves differed, the nature of the tests were much the same.

*The functions of BIOS could be expanded by special programs called device drivers. These small programs contained specific instructions which enabled BIOS to manage devices unfamiliar to it (for example, a new tape drive). Device drivers could also extend the capabilities of BIOS to manage memory. The user specified which device drivers to load by listing them in the CONFIG.SYS file.*

# How DOS Processes an Instruction

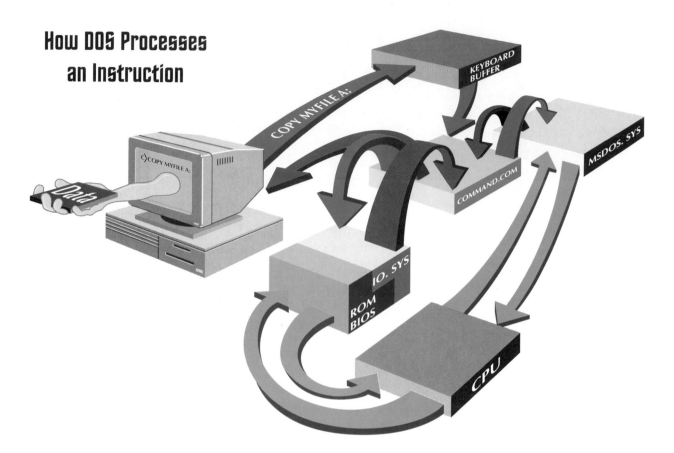

MS-DOS itself was made up of several parts. The IO.SYS operating system file was the part of the BIOS that could be improved with each version of DOS. The MSDOS.SYS file (sometimes called the *kernel*) was a basic set of operating instructions which remained in memory while the PC was "powered on." The COMMAND.COM file was a *command interpeter*—the part of DOS which translated and executed the user's commands.

Once MS-DOS was loaded (copied into RAM), it could respond to a limited number of commands such as copying, deleting, or reorganizing files on the hard disk. For example, suppose the user wanted a file copied from the hard disk to a diskette as a backup. First, the user would type the DOS command **COPY**, followed by the location of the file to be copied, followed by the location to which to copy the file. After typing the command (and pressing the Enter key to signal that the command should be executed), the user waited for the PC to execute the command. First, the keyboard microprocessor would signal the PC's CPU that keys had been pressed. The CPU would signal for ROM BIOS to translate the incoming keypresses and store them in memory. (For a fuller explanation of this procedure, refer to Chapter 1.)

Meanwhile, COMMAND.COM (the command interpeter) constantly scanned the keyboard buffer in memory, watching for the Enter key, which would signify that a command was awaiting execution. Upon recognizing that the Enter key had been pressed, COMMAND.COM would then read the entire contents of the keyboard buffer, and compare it against an internal table of valid commands. Upon finding a match for the COPY command, COMMAND.COM first verified that the the *syntax* (order of characters) was correct for the typed instruction.

To perform the COPY command, COMMAND.COM executed a series of instructions which it kept in an internal table. From time to time, while executing the instructions associated with the COPY command, COMMAND.COM would call upon MSDOS.SYS to perform some low-level functions such as

moving a file into RAM. Because the user had requested that a file be copied to a diskette, the help of the BIOS (basic input output system) was also required. The BIOS performed the input/output functions such as reading files from a diskette and writing files to the hard disk.

As you learned earlier, BIOS consisted of two parts: ROM BIOS (permanent instructions stored on a microchip) and IO.SYS (upgradable instructions contained in an electronic file stored on the hard disk). IO.SYS interpeted the instructions contained within ROM BIOS and added additional instructions, so standardized function calls could use ROM. This was necessary because ROM BIOS chips varied from PC to PC. IO.SYS interpeted the differences for the rest of the MS-DOS operating system.

Memory for the main computer cores of a starship consists of 2,048 dedicated processing modules. Each processing module is comprised of 144 isolinear chips. The storage capacity of each module varies, depending on the type and structure of the data currently stored within it. LCARS utilizes a free-flowing data management system, organizing data with whatever method optimizes both storage capacity and data retrieval. However, the storage capacity of most processing modules averages 630,000 kiloquads of information.

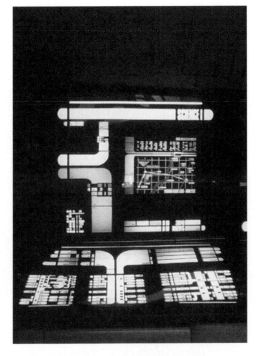

*LCARS manages many different types of data (such as the planetary analysis shown here), determining the optimal storage format for each type.*

# How MS-DOS Managed Memory

Application programs placed themselves in memory to run, and used additional RAM to prepare requests for processing by the CPU. When a PC user started a program, that program made an initial request from DOS for as much memory as it needed. During execution, the program often requested more memory; as long as memory was available, DOS would allocate it to the program. If additional memory was not available, the program would often simply stop running, or it would issue some kind of error message (such as "Insufficient memory").

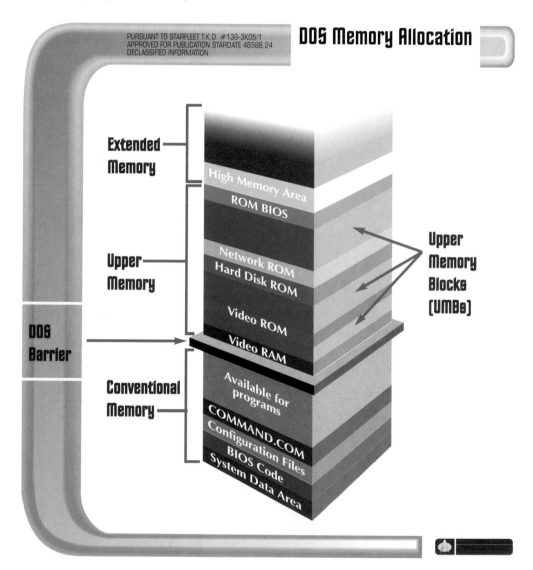

**DOS Memory Allocation**

PURSUANT TO STARFLEET T.K.O. #136-3K05/1
APPROVED FOR PUBLICATION STARDATE 46588.24
DECLASSIFIED INFORMATION

Extended Memory

High Memory Area

ROM BIOS

Network ROM

Hard Disk ROM

Upper Memory

Video ROM

Video RAM

DOS Barrier

Upper Memory Blocks (UMBs)

Conventional Memory

Available for programs

COMMAND.COM

Configuration Files

BIOS Code

System Data Area

In the course of using a program, the user created data files; these were kept in RAM until saved to a storage medium such as the hard disk. If the user created large data files, the program required larger amounts of RAM to manipulate the data. When the user exited (shut down) a program, DOS freed the memory it had previously allocated. This made room for the next program the user might want to run.

MS-DOS directly managed the PC's first megabyte of RAM. That 1 MB (1,048,576 bytes) was divided into two sections: one acted as a working area for programs, and the other for DOS's own use. *Conventional memory* (from 0K to 640K) was the primary working area for programs. The *DOS barrier*, as it came to be known, divided conventional (lower) memory from *upper memory* (640K to 1MB, also called system memory), which was reserved for use by DOS. Most PCs had more than 1MB of memory. DOS could not access this additional memory directly, but specially designed programs could. This additional memory was called *extended memory*—you'll learn more about extended memory in the sections that follow.

DOS's original designers assumed that programs for personal computers would never need more than 64K of memory, so they did not make provision for it. As additional memory became needed, a switching system was devised whereby data was switched in and out of ten "banks" of RAM (64K each) for a total of 640K. Even after this method was no longer necessary, the 640K boundary had to be maintained in later versions of MS-DOS, to keep them capable of running older

programs. This was called "maintaining compatibility."

Conventional memory, as it was originally designed, was supposed to hold all the instructions required for the computer to run. As these basic instructions grew more complex, they required more RAM. Following the development of "high memory" (discussed later in this chapter), some of these control programs and device drivers could be moved there. Even so, not all of the rather limited 640K of conventional memory was actually available for use by user programs.

*Conventional Memory*

When the PC was booted, three files were copied from the hard drive (or a diskette in drive A) into conventional memory: COMMAND.COM, MSDOS.SYS and IO.SYS. Together with ROM BIOS, these three files comprised the PC's operating system. After DOS was loaded, an area in conventional memory was set up for keeping track of open files. This area was called the *system data area*. Next, device drivers were copied into

conventional memory. In addition, any specific configuration requests from CONFIG.SYS were also loaded during the booting process. After DOS was loaded, less conventional memory remained for use by user programs. The amount could be as high as 620K, or as low as 420K, depending on the DOS version used.

## Upper Memory

The area above conventional memory between 640K and 1MB was called *upper memory*. User programs could not use this area—it was considered "reserved." Upper memory was the area where DOS stored its BIOS.

*Upper Memory*

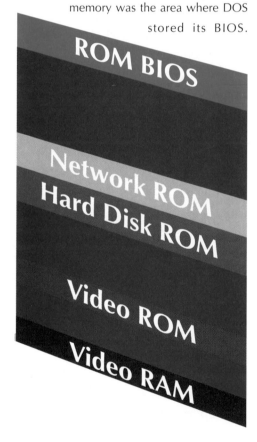

There was also an area in upper memory called *video RAM*; images were placed here before they were displayed on the monitor. In later incarnations of the PC, video RAM became physically relocated to the *video expansion card*, for exclusive use by that card and not by the CPU or DOS.

DOS left many areas of upper memory generally unused. These areas were called *UMBs*, or **U**pper **M**emory **B**locks. An upper-memory device driver enabled DOS to make these unused areas available for certain specialized programs—that way, those same programs could be loaded into upper memory blocks, instead of using valuable conventional memory. UMBs were used by two different types of programs: device drivers and *TSRs* (**t**erminate-and-**s**tay-**r**esident programs). These two types of small program fit easily into the unused areas. Device drivers you have already learned about; they enable DOS to interact with ancillary hardware such as a mouse. TSRs were special utility programs that were loaded into memory and left dormant until the user pressed specific keys to activate them. TSRs were usually simple tools (such as a calculator or a notepad) which could be used without exiting the larger program that was actively running. A portion of these TSRs ran at all times, monitoring their designated *interrupt signal* to see if the user or some other computer process was calling them.

114

## Extended Memory

*Extended Memory* was the memory above the 1MB mark. If a PC had a total of 4MB of RAM, 3MB of that memory was extended memory. In order to use extended memory, a special device driver, called an *extended memory manager*, was loaded into RAM. When DOS was running in its normal operating mode, called *real mode*, the CPU could not access extended memory. DOS had a fixed number of memory addresses, and in real mode, each address represented an actual memory address between 0K to 1MB.

In order to address memory areas above 1MB, the CPU had to be switched to another mode called *protected mode*. Here, the CPU was able to create additional addresses for memory above 1MB. These addresses were accessed through the extended memory manager, of which DOS was unaware. (Remember that DOS could not handle memory addresses above 1MB.) In simplest terms, the extended memory manager "turned on" additional memory addresses within the CPU, and managed their use. Programs had to be written specifically to use extended memory; they had to know how to access the extended memory manager (and through it, the memory addresses above 1 MB).

*"Starfleet computer engineers tend to think of an operating system as a human interface to the machine, whereas with every computer or android system I've ever worked with, the operating system is the machine's personality, the thing that makes it take flight, rather than the thing which displays a bunch of text and diagrams at you. There is no true reason why the role of the machine in our lives should be maintained as merely an appliance. A real operating system should allow machines to speak directly to you—that's why I made my machines like people. A real operating system should be communicative, intelligent, and intuitive, and if that means giving machines sentience, then so be it."*

**—Excerpt from A Life in the Machine: An Essay in Twelve Volumes on the Applications of Computer Science, by Dr. Noonian Soong, CSD, Professor Emeritus, Cygnian Institute for Advanced Cybernetics.**

*"A real operating system should allow machines to speak directly to you."*

**—Excerpted from "Often Wrong: My Life and Times" by Dr. Noonian Soong.**

One might wonder why the DOS designers did not simply scrap real mode when it became limiting. The answer was compatibility. For better or worse, the makers of DOS were committed to keeping their product compatible with all programs designed for previous versions of DOS. This practice was known as *downward compatibility*. As you will learn shortly, however, software designers found innovative ways to circumvent the limitations of real mode.

## High Memory Area

The first 64K of extended memory was called the *high memory area,* or *HMA*. This area was first made available on PCs with the Intel 80286 microprocessor, and remained so with later-model CPUs. DOS could access this area directly, with the help of a *high memory area device driver*. This driver enabled any program written for the HMA to use it, although most programs chose not to. Because the HMA was typically left alone, it became a safe area in which to place DOS. By moving DOS to the HMA, more conventional memory could be made available for user programs.

## Expanded Memory

Like extended memory, *expanded memory* could not be used for running programs, *but only for storing program data temporarily*. However, unlike extended memory, expanded memory could be reached by DOS *directly*, with the help of an *expanded memory device driver*. Extended memory was not accessed through DOS; instead, an extended memory manager rerouted requests for memory (without DOS' knowledge) to memory addresses above 1 MB. Expanded memory, on the other hand, was accessed by DOS through a special area located in upper memory.

Expanded memory, unlike extended memory, was accessed without forcing the CPU to run in protected mode, and without creating an "extended" set of extra memory addresses.

The gateway to expanded memory was through an unused area of upper memory called a *page frame*. This was a 64K area created by the expanded memory device driver. Data was copied from expanded memory into the page frame for processing, and then back to expanded memory.

From our privileged position in time, twentieth-century operating systems may seem more complex than was strictly necessary. Some of this complexity was an inevitable concession to compatibility. The resulting consistency kept the early computers useful. They served their era well, especially in light of diverse software they were able to support.

# Expanded Memory

PURSUANT TO STARFLEET T.K.O. #136-3K05/1
APPROVED FOR PUBLICATION STARDATE 46588.24
DECLASSIFIED INFORMATION

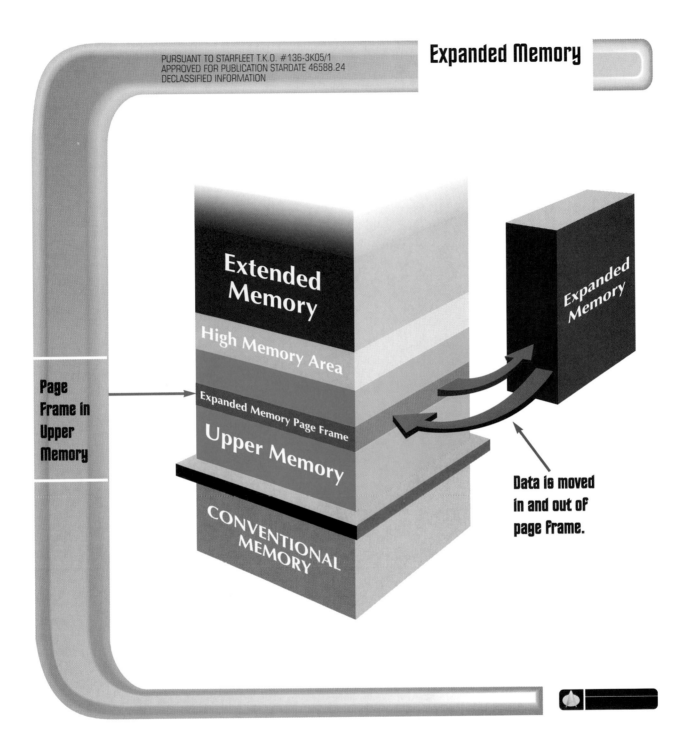

**Page Frame in Upper Memory**

Extended Memory

High Memory Area

Expanded Memory Page Frame

Upper Memory

CONVENTIONAL MEMORY

Expanded Memory

**Data is moved in and out of page frame.**

117

# The Role of Software

Computer systems in use throughout the Federation "create" programs on the fly in response to varying user requests. In contrast, twentieth century PCs operated under a system where the user's needs were separated from the needs of the PC itself (the need to store, retrieve, and organize data, while interacting with an abundance of hardware). The needs of the PC were handled by the operating system, and as such, the operating system was usually purchased with the PC. The needs of the user were met by various user programs called applications. Each user had a different set of specific needs, so applications were sold separately from the PC and its operating system. Because users were free to add new applications at any time, it was easy to expand the capability of individual PCs.

Applications were written using a *programming language*. Most programming languages allowed a programmer to code the instructions for an application without understanding the PC's complex low-level, internal language. Once the instructions were written, a separate program was used to reinterpret the high-level instructions, and *compile* them into low-level instructions. The process of compiling caused the programmer's instructions (which usually resembled a shorthand form of written language) to be converted into the 1's and 0's of the PC's own *machine language*. After being compiled, the resulting program file was ready for the user to execute (run) by simply causing the PC's operating system to load that program file it into memory.

*Software* was a term which referred to programmed instructions and it included both operating system software, and user software (applications). Software was the opposite of *hardware*, which included the actual equipment which comprised a PC system: the monitor, system unit, keyboard, modem, printer, etc. *Operating system software* was a specialized category of software that included a variety of control programs for the PC, such as DOS (an operating system), Windows (an operating environment), and NetWare (a network operating system). They responded not only to users' commands, but also to requests from user programs.

Once a PC had its system software installed, it was ready to run *application software* (also known simply as "applications" or "user programs"). Each application software processed a specific type of data for the user; additional applications were purchased to process other types of data. A typical application was designed in an entirely generalized fashion—although each application was designed for a specific purpose, it was done in such a way which allowed some flexibility to the user. A user's commands to an application were not given generally (using spoken languages), but specifically—using a coded language (in the form of keystrokes) designed for only the application itself. The same keystrokes were not generally used to control the same functions within other applications.

Software development was a fiercely competitive industry, and programs were sold for every level of user. For example, in the "word processing" category (programs for writing and editing), dozens of available applications performed the same basic functions—but at differing levels of complexity. A user who did not require the elaborate "high-level" functions needed for publishing books did not have to pay for them. She could purchase a simple, inexpensive application.

When a user shopped for an application, she not only had to look at the features it offered, but also the *system resources* (storage and memory) it required. The more features an application contained, the more resources it needed. For example, a word processing program with only basic features might require only 640K of memory and 2MB of hard disk space, while a feature-rich word processing program might require 4MB of memory and 12MB of hard disk space. If her PC did not have the minimum amount of RAM and hard disk space required, the user would have a choice to make: upgrade her PC to meet the program's requirements, or purchase a program that made fewer demands on her PC's resources.

By the end of the twentieth century, so many different types of applications existed that they can not all be described in these pages. Examining several major types will, however, provide insight into the workings and uses of the twentieth century PC.

When a user started a program under MS-DOS, the application gained sole command of the PC's environment. To fulfill user requests, the application sometimes bypassed DOS, and sent its instructions directly to the CPU. More often, the application required some assistance from the operating system, in order to interact correctly with the PC's hardware. That assistance came in the form of requests to IO.SYS, a small program that was part of the BIOS ("basic input/output system").

To carry out the application's instructions, the BIOS could send requests to the CPU, or sometimes, to another part of the operating system—MSDOS.SYS. In answer to requests from the BIOS, MSDOS.SYS (in turn) often called upon the management abilities of yet another part of the operating system, COMMAND.COM.

A twentieth-century user would look in vain for "software" in a starship's computer system. Onboard a starship, when a user needs to perform a particular task, a request is made of the computer. The computer may require additional information regarding the form in which the output of the request should take; but once the computer understands what is wanted, the request is processed immediately. LCARS has the ability to assume the role of any type of "software."—in twentieth-century terms, LCARS provides a flexible "software environment" which changes depending on its user's needs, either permanently or for the moment. If the user requires optical storage output to a portable isolinear chip, it is provided, although normally LCARS displays its output on the designated control panel.

119

# How an Application Relates to the Operating System

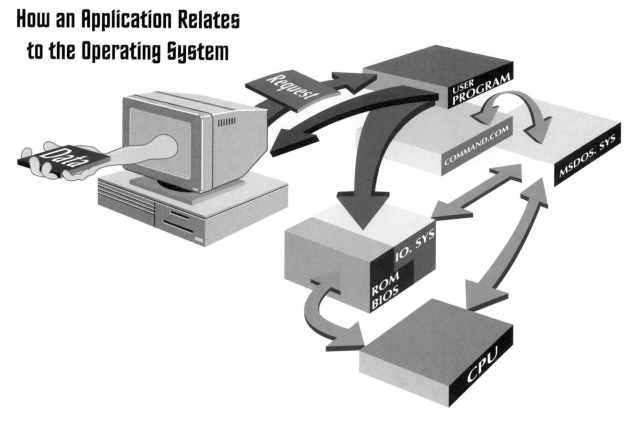

The application was usually unaware of exactly how its instructions were being carried out—it would request that a file be moved into memory or copied from disk, and it knew that it was being done—but it did not know how. The details of such low-level functions were the domain of the operating system, and one reason why it existed in the first place. Although an application could ignore the operating system and send its instructions directly to the CPU, this was not usually done because the application would not know in advance exactly what type of PC system was running it, and therefore, what types of hardware the application would need to interact with.

*In the few hours of leisure time permitted a starship captain, I often enjoy reading a printed book from my treasured store of antique bound volumes. What I find fascinating is the process involved in preparing the written word for printing. Twentieth-century word processors had to be flexible to meet the demands of all types of writers, and as such, they provided many useful "tools of the trade:" spelling checkers, grammar checkers, and complete editing capablity. LCARS can provide some of these these same services too, and I use them as a matter of course when recording permanent log records.*

—**Captain Jean-Luc Picard,**
**Ship's Captain, U.S.S. Enterprise**

**120**

# Popular Types of Applications

There were countless types of applications from which a user could choose. What follows is a brief description of each of the major types of applications that were popular at the end of the twentieth century.

A **word processor** managed words—allowing the user to enter, compose, and perfect them to form letters, memos, and reports. Word processors were programs that allowed a computer to mimic an old Earth mechanical device called a *typewriter*. Prior to the widespread use of voice recognizers, the users of word processors created paragraphs (such as the one you are reading now) by typing their text character-by-character. A feature called *word wrapping* improved the user's typing speed by eliminating typewriter-style "carriage returns." When the cursor reached the end of the line where text was currently being entered, it would jump automatically to the beginning of the next line, wrapping the words from one line to the next. If words were later inserted or deleted, the text that followed the edit was adjusted automatically. Word processors, thus, provided an easy means for creating and editing written documents.

**Spreadsheet programs** were used to manipulate columns of numbers, creating complex calculations and analyses. A spreadsheet appeared on-screen as a matrix of *columns* and *rows*; the intersection of a column and a row formed a *cell*. Columns were identified

by letters, and rows were identified by numbers. The *address* of a cell—the relative location of its contents—combined the letter of a column with the number of a row, as in **G11**. Cell addresses were important because they formed the building blocks for *formulas*. For example, to add the contents of three cells, the user might enter a formula such as this:

**=B2+C2+D2**

The inherent "interconnectedness" of a spreadsheet was considered one of its more powerful features. The totals of several cells could be added to another total later in the spreadsheet, creating subtotals and grand totals. If the contents of a single cell changed, the dependent totals were recalculated automatically. Thus, spreadsheet programs made it easy to perform complex calculations and "what if" analyses.

A **database** was a collection of interrelated *records*. For example, the Starfleet personnel file for a single individual would be seen as a single record, while the combination of personnel files for an entire starship would be seen as a *database*. The pieces of data comprising a single record (such as a person's name, rank, and serial number) would be seen as *fields*. Records could be sorted within the database using a *key field*, a single field within a record that identifies it in some way. For example, a Starfleet personnel database could be sorted by

**121**

name, rank, planet of origin, or any other key field. Using a *query language* incorporated into the database program, a user could create custom reports and analyses using information pulled from the database. Late in the twentieth century, databases began to track more than simply written records. For example, a photo of an employee could be kept in the database along with that person's employment record. Signatures could be scanned in and then stored—these signatures could later be used in security systems. Voice annotations, graphics, and even video (digitized audio-visual recordings) could be incorporated into databases, although such databases required large amounts of hard disk storage.

**Desktop publishing** programs excelled in the manipulation of text and graphics; which allowed a user to give a document "the authority of print." With a desktop publishing program, a user maintained total control over the position of both text and graphics images on the page. Text could be placed in columns, or *wrapped* around photographic or other images with precision. When using a desktop publishing program, text was normally created using a word processor, and graphics were created using a "painting" or "drawing" program. These separate files were then combined, using the precise tools of the desktop publishing program. As more users took advantage of this technique, more amateur documents gained a "polished" look. By the end of the century, most commercial publishers were using the more elaborate versions of desktop publishing.

A **paint program** allowed the user to create an illustration pixel by pixel (the smallest logical unit of the display). The illustration was then modified by changing individual pixels. A paint program each illustration as a *bitmap* (pattern of pixels which comprised the object). Enlarging or shrinking an image in a paint program often created distortion. For example, when an object was enlarged to twice its size, each single pixel in the original drawing became four pixels—often resulting in jagged outlines and a loss of detail. Paint programs were the first to employ a graphic control device called a *toolbar*. It contained small pictographic symbols representing various tools that could be used to draw simple objects—particularly circles, ellipses, rectangles, rounded rectangles, and polygons. Additional tools on the toolbar simulated some of the traditional Earth tools used for painting and drawing—paintbrush, spray can, pencil, and eraser.

**Drawing programs** offered an alternative to the *bit-mapped graphics* of paint programs. A drawing program stored objects not as bitmaps, but as a complex series of mathematical formulas called *vectors*. These formulas contained information on the exact specifications for each object: its size, position in the illustration, and its perspective. Because elements in a drawing program were treated as complex mathematical formulas, there was no distortion when they were resized. Instead, the object's dimensions were adjusted in the formula. Drawing programs contained sophisticated tools for manipulating the objects that made up an illustration. These tools enabled the user to rotate an object (pivot on its center point), change its perspective, *extrude* it (add depth), and *mirror* it (flip it on its vertical axis). In addition, drawing programs typically featured coloring and shading tools of considerable sophistication.

One special type of program, *virus programs*, were the type of twentieth-century application that a user did not buy, but acquired unwittingly by obtaining "infected" files from another PC system. The sole purpose of a virus was not to serve the user's needs, but to infiltrate a user's system. Some computer viruses were benign, but most were especially destructive, overwriting data files, program files, and even the operating system itself.

*Unfortunately, viruses are not manifestations of a distant past. The Enterprise was tracing the last remants of the mythical Iconian race when our computers were infected by a virus. This incident occured when we downloaded the computer logs of the U.S.S. Yamato, which had unknowingly to us also been infected. When I was sent to investigate the problem, I myself became infected with this virus. Eventually my self-correction program eradicated any occurence of the virus within my positronic neural net, although I must admit that being neurologically infected was not a pleasant experience.*

**—Lt. Commander Data, Operations Manager, U.S.S. Enterprise**

*"Being neurologically infected by a computer virus was not a pleasant experience."*
**—Lt. Commander Data, U.S.S. Enterprise**

*Today, a user does not purchase a program, but she designs it, verbally or through control panel input, by specifically requesting exactly what is needed. LCARS packages its information based on these requests, displaying the requested data in a format that the user prefers. This format transcends all categorical forms of media. LCARS is capable of rendering its output in a purely linear, binary form, for reception by alien computing devices. Advanced species who communicate over telepathic frequencies can interact with LCARS by means of standardized mental archetypes. Humans, Vulcans, Klingons, and the other natural-language-speaking members of the Federation may employ a variety of media when communicating with LCARS—even several media simultaneously, as shown by a holodeck simulation.*

**—Dr. Leah Brahms, Starfleet Design Engineer**

**Chapter** | **Ten**

# Emerging Technologies of the Late Twentieth Century

By studying the technological advances of a particular race, you can discover so much about its culture and sociology. For example, the Bynars' social pairing and their language are defined by the level of computer technology they enjoy. The lack of original technology among the Pakleds reflects their lack of inventiveness, although their ability to acquire technology from other races is a testiment to their ingenuity (and lack of ethics). My own race, the Betazoids, do not have a long list of technological achievements—we are more concerned with the development of our telepathic powers. Many emerging technologies of the late twentieth century influenced the development of computers themselves, and of social developments dependent upon computer technology. No study of twentieth-century personal computers would be complete without the inclusion of these influences.

*—Lt. Commander Deanna Troi,*
*Counselor, U.S.S. Enterprise*

# Robots and Cybernetics

Historical studies have theorized that robotic components were first being developed on Earth in the United States prior to the First World War (calendar year 1917), though much of the paperwork substantiating such theories has been lost. Robots were first developed successfully on Earth in 1959. These robots were first deployed commercially in manufacturing and heavy industry; they were equipped with little more than a programmable mechanical arm. One of the first commercial robots was called Unimate, and it was used by General Motors (a manufacturer of personal vehicles powered by combustion engines) to perform die-casting tasks. Unimate was manufactured by a company called Unimation, and was capable of performing 180 separate steps.

By 1969, free-standing *locomotion robots* had been developed. One of the first of these new breed of robots was Shakey, the first fully mobile robot with artificial intelligence.

## Shakey—One of the First Mobile Robots

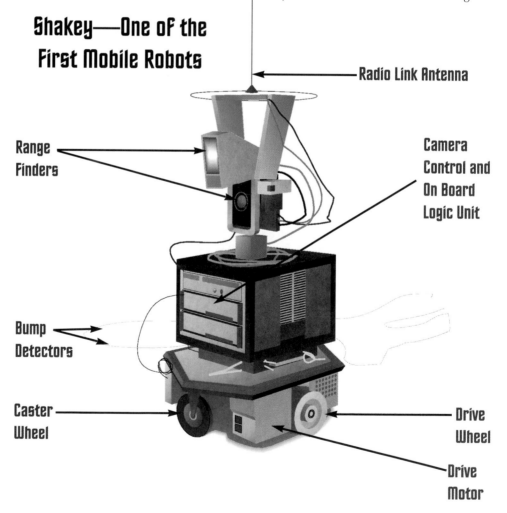

Radio Link Antenna

Range Finders

Camera Control and On Board Logic Unit

Bump Detectors

Caster Wheel

Drive Wheel

Drive Motor

Shakey was capable of making decisions by means of an on-board logic unit. A television camera served as Shakey's "eyes"—but this system proved notoriously unreliable in navigating obstacles, so *bump detectors* (tiny wire coils) were employed to prevent Shakey from running into objects. The Stanford Research Laboratories apparently did not construct Shakey from a complete blueprint, as evidenced by the hand-sawed wooden planks used to hold up its radio antenna.

By the 1980s, robots were widely employed in place of human workers, performing many tedious or dangerous jobs. This allowed these same human workers to perform tasks that required more intelligence— tasks that robots could not yet be programmed to perform. The major problem that robotics engineers faced was the task of creating mechanisms that could emulate accurately the function of sense organs. By the end of the twentieth century, robot sensors were limited to five types: *tactile, range, proximity, acoustic,* and *visual.*

*Many of Data's senses, including motor control, surpass that of most humaniods.*

Although Lt. Commander Data was designed to resemble a human being, many of his senses surpass those of most humanoids. Data's auditory sensors monitor all wavelengths well into the ultrasonic frequencies. Low frequencies of only a few decibels are equally as clear as high frequencies. Data's visual sensors are similarly sensitive, detecting lightwaves on both ends of the spectrum, from infared to ultraviolet. Motor skills, such as eye-to-hand coordination, are simulated with a combination of pneumatic tubes, nano-tactile sensors, electromagnetic auratic detectors, and isolinear-controlled pressure pads.

Tactile sensors told these early robots whether they were touching an object, how tightly they were gripping an object, the shape of an object, and even whether an object was slipping from their grasp. Touch sensors, embedded in the fingertips of a robot, were comprised of individual microswitches that were triggered when a robot's hand closed over an object. Pressure switches transmitted relative values to the robot's logic unit, indicating the amount of pressure being applied to an object. Many robot gripping surfaces used what was then called a "sensor array" (not to be confused with a starship's telemetry systems): a group of individual tactile elements, any of which could be activated at a given time.

In twentieth-century robots, range sensors determined the distance between the sensor and the target object; proximity sensors determined the presence of specific objects. The main difference between them was that range sensors usually measured longer distances than proximity sensors. Both types used similar methods of distance detection. Light detectors measured the light reflected from an object; based on the amount of reflected light, the robot could calculate the distance between itself and the object. Magnetic and eddy-current sensors (which could detect a change in magnetic field strength) were used to probe for the presence of metals. Acoustic sensors measured reflected sound waves to determine the robot's distance to an object. By analyzing the changes in the reflected wave, the robot could determine an object's surface traits, dimensions, and even its shape.

Machine vision systems were among the most sophisticated sensors installed in robots of the late twentieth century. These systems were, however, very limited; they were used mostly for locating, identifying, and counting tasks. While there were many types of machine vision systems, most incorporated a camera type developed for an early form of electronic visual communication (*television*). The camera produced an analog visual image, which was then converted into a digital image. The robot then analyzed this image, comparing it with other digital images stored in memory. This process was called *template matching*. An alternative process was called *feature analysis*: the robot would analyze the digital image to determine its dimension, area, orientation, and other distinguishing features.

One of the more unconventional researchers in the field of robotics on twentieth-century Earth was Rodney Brooks. Although his robots were not used in many practical operations, his improvements in robot sensory systems led to the development of more conventional robots for use in homes, businesses, medical technology, and early space exploration. Brooks' team created robots of varied shape, size, and function, though the exact meaning of the names is lost to antiquity. "Herbert" gathered aluminum beverage cans from desktops. "Squirt" was a small mechanical insect (whose design, nevertheless, does not suggest the ejection of fluid). With such intimidating names as "Genghis" and "Atilla," Brooks' more famous mechanical bugs—designed in part by graduate student Colin Angle—roamed around rooms, navigating obstacles and sometimes even "stalking" human beings. Their behavior was surprisingly complex for brainless machines.

Rodney Brooks did not worry about endowing his robots with a true artificial intelligence; he felt there was no need to give robots human intelligence in the first place. According to Brooks, robots could be useful when given an intelligence only on a par with an insect's. In fact, most of the robots that Brooks built were designed to mimic some type of insect. He envisioned tiny insect-like robots, injected into the human bloodstream and programmed to repair clogged arteries. (His contributions made that dream a reality in the twenty-second century.)

Most robots built at the end of the twentieth century were designed to handle specific tasks. Transitions Research Corporation, for example, built a robotic nurse, designed to navigate from floor to floor in a large hospital, delivering meals to hospital beds, and shuffling small payloads (such as medical records, pharmaceuticals, or blood samples) from one department to another.

*The definition of "life" is a difficult one, and one that has troubled mankind for millennia. I was once ordered to act as the Prosecutor in a trial against Lt. Commander Data, which was based on that very question. Was Data "alive", or was he simply a sophisticated machine? Having served with him, I had no doubt he was alive; but I almost proved myself wrong. Secretly, I must confess that I was very glad when I lost the case.*

**—Commander William T. Riker, Executive Officer, U.S.S. Enterprise**

# Artificial Intelligence

*In the act of programming an android, it is very easy for a person in my position to begin to assume the role of a god. I therefore suffer, at times, from the delusion that every element of code or mechanical engineering that I create is manifestly perfect. On more than one occasion, a creation has stared back at me in the face with pronounced imperfection. A software program, no matter how expertly coded, is rarely perfect on the first try. When I built my first android, I wrote an artificial emotion program to endow my creation with a sense of humanity. The program proved less than perfect, and I was forced to dismantle my creation because it was too erratic.*

**—Excerpted from "Often Wrong: My Life and Times" by Dr. Noonian Soong**

The twentieth century saw its first applications of *artificial intelligence* in three major areas: *application* (the use of artificially-intelligent machines in business and industry), *cognitive science* (a study in the workings of natural intelligence—the brain), and *simulation* (an investigation into the best ways to produce intelligence in a computer).

Artificial intelligence (AI) techniques of the twentieth century were divided into *symbolic* and *non-symbolic* approaches. The symbolic view was represented by programmers of rule-based systems called *expert systems* that manipulated discrete symbols according to specific rules, in order to determine a result. The symbolic view worked best in situations where problems could be reduced to a set of questions with yes/no answers—or to quantifiable degrees, amounts, or ratings.

*Prof. Moriarty and his companion lived a real "life" inside a complex holodeck simulation.*

 *Professor Moriarty, a holodeck creation, became "self-aware" as the result of a malfunction. He displayed a unique brand of "artificial intelligence," even to the point of asserting he must be made "real." He held the Enterprise hostage and ordered us to devise a method to allow him to "live" with his companion outside the holodeck. We were not able to fulfill his demands of course, but we were able to give them a sort of "real" life in a complex holodeck simulation of which they are thankfully unaware.*
—**Commander William T. Riker, Executive Officer, U.S.S. Enterprise**

The first step in building an expert system was to define a set of rules, and then program them. These rules were, for the most part, *conditional* in nature ("if *x*, then *y*"); reducing them mathematically into *comparative logic formulas* was relatively easy.

People used expert systems as though they were consultants with expertise in performing a particular task, or in executing their job. In fact, a database of rules was needed to program an expert system. Creating it required interviewing actual living consultants and recording their answers. Symbolic AI showed its weaknesses, however, when presented with situations that could not be defined easily in terms of its rules.

## Neural Networks

The non-symbolic view was represented in large part by *programmers of neural networks*. This approach to AI considered intelligence not as a symbol-processing mechanism, but rather as a vast collection of *nodes*. These nodes were neural network components designed to emulate the processes of connected neurons within the human brain.

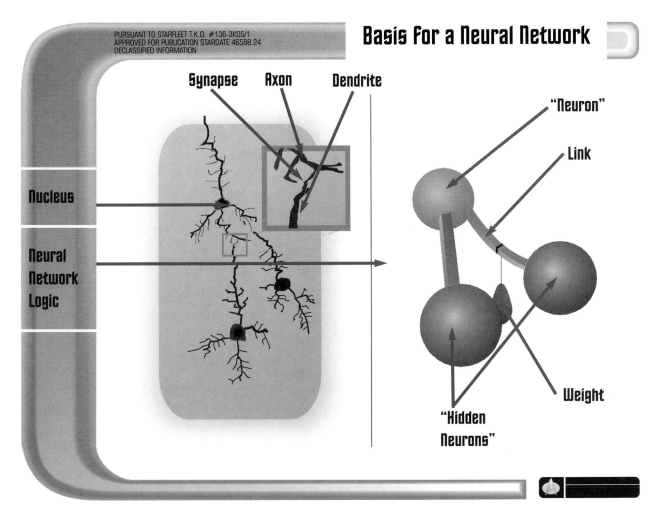

PURSUANT TO STARFLEET T.K.O. #136-3K05/1
APPROVED FOR PUBLICATION STARDATE 46588.24
DECLASSIFIED INFORMATION

## Basis for a Neural Network

Synapse  Axon  Dendrite

"Neuron"

Link

Nucleus

Neural Network Logic

"Hidden Neurons"

Weight

The human brain is itself a huge mass of connected cells forming a network of incredible complexity. Each of these cells (*neurons*) gather input from other cells to which they're connected, and generate output based on the strengths of the inputs. The main body of a cell is called the *nucleus*. Neurons send signals to and from other neurons through thin branches called *dendrites* and *axons*. Dendrites conduct signals *to* the main cell body; *axons* conduct signals *from* it. When these signals are strong enough, the neuron will "fire"—sending an electrochemical pulse (*neurotransmission*) from the cell's body, down the axon, and out into the *synapse*, the connection between neurons. A neural network was a program designed to emulate the brain cells' complex interrelationship.

A *neural network* was comprised of many nodes; each representing a single "neuron." Each node was interconnected with other nodes through a series of program instructions which mimicked the action of neurons in the human brain. Each numerical value the node received as input was multiplied by a *weighting factor*. All the node's inputs were then totaled. If this sum was greater than the node's *threshold value*, the node "fired," sending input to the next nodes in the network. In a simple neural network, the output of a node was 1 if it "fired," and 0 if it did not "fire."

Neural networks incorporated no fewer than three layers of nodes. The first of these represented the *input layer*—the source of the network's input. The signals from the input nodes were processed and passed onto the *hidden layer*, of which there was at least one, though possibly several more sub-layers or "slabs." In the hidden layer(s), the signals were combined mathematically with patterns left by prior signals. The results from the hidden layer were then passed on to the *output layer*. The pattern generated by the output layer was the network's result.

*Backpropagation neural networks* were often used in character recognition. The letter "A" in "Times Roman font" (a style of type used widely in publishing) looked noticeably different from the letter "A" in "Courier font" (a type style mimicking that of a typewriter). In a process called *training*, many examples of the letter "A"—in vastly differing type styles—were fed into a neural network. The network evaluated its own output, and modified the strength of certain connections (nodes) such that future output would be more accurate. Eventually, the neural network "learned" to recognize the letter "A" in many different type styles. The output of such a network was never "Yes" or "No"—instead, a numerical value that represented the likelihood of the result.

What made neural networks powerful was that they could be trained to "weight" their own connections. As with other types of networks, the architecture of a neural network was called its *topology*; in one such design, the neural network program provided sample input to the network, and then compared the output of the network with the desired result. If the result was deemed incorrect (or too dissimilar to the output thus far to be possibly correct), the weighting factor was modified. A formula called *backpropagation* would bring the next output result closer to the desired result. If the user provided the neural network with many input samples, the network would modify its own interconnections each time, producing more accurate results. The result of a neural network's calculations always fell somewhere between a "definite yes" and "definite no." These in-between values were interpreted as percentages of probability—its resemblence to known patterns.

Although the output of a neural network was generally quite accurate—and capable of becoming more accurate over time—such results could not be explained to the user in any form. The "reasons" behind the neural network's selection of its "best guess" could not be explained in any meaningful way. By contrast, an *expert system* kept a running tally of what rules were used in the formation of its projections and recommendations. During the last decade of the twentieth century, neural networks were used in large part by financial institutions, which had a great need for accurate prediction of future economic and financial trends. (This need compelled many financial analysts to resort to such forecasting methods—which were at least scientific, even if non-economic.) Neural nets also found use in medical research laboratories, helping researchers isolate diseases and viruses from complex laboratory cultures.

## Fuzzy Logic

By the end of the 1900s, computers had begun to address problems that could not be answered with a binary "Yes" or "No." *Fuzzy logic* was a programming method that meant to take into account the many ambiguities present in the real world. The relative temperature in a room (is it "too hot," "too cold," or "just right"?) is just one example of the huge amount of "fuzzy" data with which the mind must deal. As another example, suppose you were trying to decide *how many workers* you should use to produce the *optimal number of widgets*, in order to maximize profits. Because it was programmed to deal with such uncertainties, a computer utilizing fuzzy logic was better able to assist its users with real-world problems.

Neural networks had a simpler task than fuzzy logic systems; they processed quantifiable data to produce a single "best guess" result. In contrast, a *fuzzy logic system* used fuzzy inputs to produce results with varying degrees of uncertainty. Logic normally used in a computer (called Boolean logic) resulted in simple "yes" and "no" answers. By contrast, the Boolean comparisons AND, OR, and NOT—when used in a fuzzy logic system—caused the fuzzy input data to be sorted into *sets* that stood for various degrees between "yes" and "no." These fuzzy sets of data produced a weighted, more precise answer.

With fuzzy logic, all things were a matter of degree. All input data was regarded as falling within a given range, but that range was non-specific. For example, at any given moment during its flight, an airplane (a fixed-wing atmospheric transport) could be said to be flying at "normal altitude," "too high," or "too low." The range for "normal altitude" could not be specified absolutely as (for example) 1000 to 2000 meters. While such a range would be adequate for flight over level ground, the same value could be suddenly "too low" if a high mountain loomed ahead.

One early application of fuzzy logic was in traffic control. The combustion-powered ground vehicles of the later 1900s traveled paved roadways which intersected at various points. Traffic at these intersecting points was governed by a timed lighting system: green for "Go," and red for "Stop." Rather than changing color at fixed intervals, a traffic system controlled by fuzzy logic could adjust to real traffic conditions. It would understand that when the traffic became too congested in a particular direction, the light should remain green for a longer period, allowing the traffic to flow at a quickened pace. Likewise, when traffic from a particular direction was uncongested, the light could remain red for a longer period of time, allowing traffic from the other direction an opportunity to move through the intersection without stopping. The duration of each green-red light cycle was governed by a combination of several similar fuzzy logic "rules" to determine the best course of action.

Fuzzy logic gained new applications rapidly. It was soon used to control the speed of underground public transports called *subways*, so that they stopped and started more smoothly. In *speech recognition systems*, the same approach allowed a computer to recognize various patterns of spoken language. In the publicly-owned trading system called the *stock market,* fuzzy logic helped investors make financial investment decisions. In a typical portable *video camera* (a recording device which captured live action and sound and stored it on magnetic tape), fuzzy logic was used to compensate for low-light and variable focus conditions, improving the quality of the recorded image.

Twentieth-century aircraft carried a "black box" (an in-flight recorder); if the black box malfunctioned just before the airplane crashed it might not record the exact position and altitude of the aircraft just prior to the crash. Using fuzzy logic, however, an investigator could determine the plane's altitude (as nearly as possible) at any point along its flight path. Data representing observed altitude changes during the flight could be submitted to a fuzzy logic system. There the data would be sorted into sets based on degrees of difference ("normal" versus "too high" or "too low"). With fuzzy inputs such as "the plane was relatively low," a *fuzzy logic algorithm* could generate a decision that matched (almost perfectly) the actual location of the plane thirteen seconds before the crash.

Such accuracy was possible because, even though the input to a fuzzy logic system was not clearly defined, it did have *range limits*—for instance, how low is "high," and how high can "high" be? The degree of "fuzzification" of the inputs was a known value, and that value played a distinct role in determining the final decision. Using a fuzzy logic system was like being uncertain about something, but knowing just how uncertain you were (the percentage of uncertainty).

# Artificial Life

   *Since the twentieth century, mankind has struggled with questions such as these: "What is life?" "Are artificial life forms actually alive?" and "Do artificial life forms have the same right to life as human beings?" These and many other questions are much debated even to this day, and the answers aren't as obvious as one might think. When I tried to prove that artificial beings such as Commander Data deserve the same rights and privileges as naturally sentient life forms, I found it a very difficult challenge. I argued that all beings are "created," and yet they are not owned by their creator. It was decided that Data possessed free will, and therefore, had the right not to consent to a series of dangerous experiments in which he would have been disassembled. However, I do not think that the struggle is over—I believe that such debates will continue as long as artificial life forms exist.*

*—Captain Jean-Luc Picard, U.S.S. Enterprise*

*"All beings are created, and yet they are not the property of their creator."*

*—Captain Jean-Luc Picard*

*"The definition of life was the subject of much debate when I created my daughter, Lal."*
—**Lt. Commander Data**

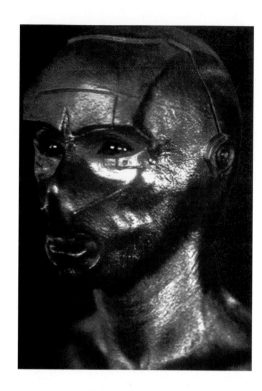

An early form of artificial life, with which even twenty-fourth century beings have had experience, is the *computer virus*. Although technically they do not qualify as "artificial life," computer viruses do boast some of the characteristics of life—most importantly, the ability to reproduce.

The study of a-life eventually led to the creation (in the early twenty-first century) of tiny robotic creatures that helped to clean up some of the pollution of the Earth's oceans. These robots "ate" certain types of chemicals or materials, reducing damaging oil spills to a form not threatening to the environment.

Although artificial life forms may be developed biologically in genetics labs, the term *artificial life* (or *a-life*) had a different use in the late twentieth century. It referred to "creatures" that existed wholly within a computer's memory. A popular computer pastime, Conway's Game of Life, was an example of the simplest computer a-life. In a computer simulation, one-celled creatures vied for living space according to a small set of mathematical rules. Much like bacteria growing in a Petri dish, "cells" within the simulation rapidly lived and died in a blur of colored patterns.

Another popular computer simulation, called SimLife, was a game in which the user created an entire biosphere populated with sophisticated life forms (including plants and animals) of his or her own design. In SimLife, the user modified each life form's genetic characteristics, or changed the environment to see what effect it had upon the creatures he or she had created. In the twentieth century it was believed in some quarters that, because the "occupants" of these computer simulations could evolve on their own, they represented an actual synthesis of life rather than just a simulation. (Keep in mind that many people of this era still believed that existence itself could be entirely explained by mathematical formulas.)

# *Virtual Reality*

*Virtual reality* was an early term for a method still used in galactic culture: the communication of computerized information using media far more advanced than a simple flat-screen monitor. Rather than communicating through text and static pictures (as was typical with PCs), virtual reality involved as many of the human senses as was feasible. It created an information-rich "environment" for users, almost as complex as natural experience. Virtual reality took users "inside" the communication channel, rather than leaving them outside looking in.

To be effective, virtual reality (VR) systems applied four basic concepts to the VR experience: viewpoint, navigation, manipulation, and immersion.

*Viewpoint* was created by simulating the position of user's eyes within a virtual (computer-created) world. In order to work, the computer needed to know where the user was located within the virtual world, and the direction he or she was facing. If the viewpoint was wrong, the entire VR experience was confusing.

*Navigation* was the process of moving the user's viewpoint from one position to another within the VR environment. When a user "moved" within the VR world, changing her viewpoint, the computer responded by displaying adjusted images based on the user's new position. Navigation was normally controlled through special eyepieces, which tracked movements of the user's eyes and calculated the approximate change in view.

*A holodeck can create a variety of artificial opponents.*

Even as early as the twenty-first century, it was known that every species needs some method of psychological "escape." For the Vulcans, that escape comes in the form of meditation. For Klingons, it comes in the form of simulated combat. The holodecks in a starship provide the crew with the means of creating their own escape—be it a quiet walk in the moonlight of Dena 4, the suspense of a Dixon Hill mystery, or anything in-between. Because of the massive memory and computing requirements in maintaining an effective illusion, the holodecks are controlled by a dedicated subsystem of the main computer core.

Two main systems comprise the holodeck itself: the *holographic imagery subsystem* (which creates the setting for the illusion), and the *matter conversion subsystem* (which uses raw materials to create physical "props"). The holographic imagery subsystem exists as a series of **o**mni-directional **h**olo **d**iodes (OHDs), of which the holodeck walls are composed. Each OHD is capable of emitting a holographic image comprised of polarized interference patterns, tailored to the position of the OHD within the holodeck. Thus, each OHD projects only its part of the desired environment.

If a likelihood exists that an object will be touched, the matter conversion subsystem replicates that object from available raw materials. These objects are as real as any other replicated object, and as such, can be removed from the holodeck if desired. When an artificial lifeform is replicated, it is given the appearance of articulation through a complex series of tractor beams.

Through *manipulation*, the user's hands joined their eyes in the virtual world. While wearing special gloves fitted with electrical connections leading to the computer, the user could reach out and pluck an object off a table. In many ways, manipulation was like viewpoint. When the user picked up an object and moved it, the object's position relative to the user's viewpoint changed.

*Immersion* was the extent to which the user was drawn into the VR world—a measure of how realistic the simulation was. With full immersion, all of the user's senses reported that she was really in the VR world. No matter where the user looked, she would see the VR world. Everything the user heard came from the VR world. The only objects the user could touch were in the VR world. Unlike a starship's holodecks, virtual reality systems of the late twentieth century were capable of only partial immersion—simulating only two senses: sight and hearing. The sense of touch (necessary for total-immersion systems) was extremely difficult to simulate in a VR environment.

To create realistic visuals, a simple VR system utilized a headset that placed a small viewing screen in front of each eye. When the user moved his or her head, the headset transmitted movement data to the computer. This data was then utilized to change the user's viewpoint by creating the appropriate images on the viewing screens.

Creating realistic sound in a VR world was a bit more complicated, given the technology available at the time. Popular sound-reproduction technology ("stereo") was capable of creating the effect of moving sounds by making the sound a little louder in one earpiece than in the other. The drawback to this technique in virtual reality was that the sound always stayed "inside" the user's head, in an area somewhere between one ear and the other. For truly realistic sound, a VR system had to be able to make sound effects appear to come not from inside the user's head, but from somewhere in the three-dimensional space of the virtual world.

After much research into the characteristics of sound waves, it was discovered that, by means of complicated mathematical formulas to make small adjustments to a digitized sound wave, sound could be made to come from any specific direction. The result of this work was a headset called the Convolvotron, a device that could create realistic sound for use in VR systems.

The most difficult sense to duplicate by way of twentieth-century technology was touch. To duplicate all the sensations detectable by the human hand proved to be one of the toughest challenges VR researchers faced. With one of several different glove-like devices, it was possible to recreate a small range of touch sensations. One type of glove employed small air bladders that inflated and deflated to apply differing amounts of pressure to parts of the hand. Another glove deployed an arrangement of pistons to apply pressure to the fingers. Still another contained special wires that, when heated, simulated the feel of different textures. These first attempts at simulating the sense of touch were a step in the right direction. It was not until the early twenty-first century, however, that touch technology developed to the point of providing a convincing illusion.

## Fractals

*Fractals* were mathematical formulas that were used to simulate the appearance of natural shapes, such as fern leaves or mountainous terrain. These shapes were said to demonstrate a trait called *self-similarity*. Basically, a shape with self-similarity shows the same details at varying magnifications. Continental coastlines were a classic example of this phenomenon. Looking at a coastline from space, the shapes caused by the coastline's roughness could be seen. Moving closer to the coastline, more detail could be seen, but this detail would take on many of the characteristics of the full coastline. A peninsula, for example, would have its own "coastline" with shape properties similar to the larger coastline. A boulder on the peninsula—and even a grain of sand adhering to the boulder—would demonstrate the same phenomenon of self-similarity.

*A fractal-created world.*

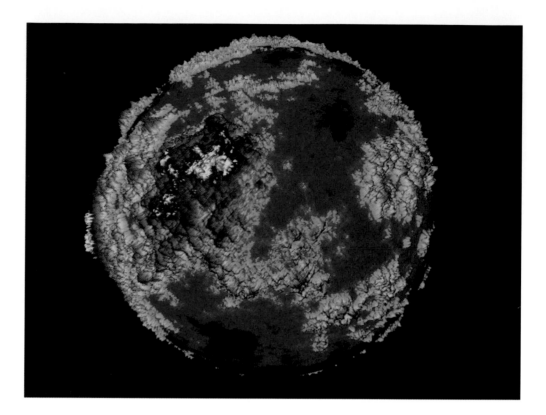

Clouds and mountain ranges are two other natural fractal-type curves. Their self-similarity was due in large part to the human mind's inability to see definitive patterns in natural phenomena. For example, to the mind's eye, a mountain range has the rough shape of a pyramid—the sharpness of its contour almost too complex for the mind to capture in a single glance, so it is ignored. Since it is equally incapable of detecting such patterns in artificial phenomena such as fractal images, the mind considers these two "unexplainable" types of images as though they were similar to one another.

Benoit Mandelbrot, a twentieth-century mathematician, noticed the self-similar characteristic of many natural shapes, and began to study them in detail. He called these self-similar curves "fractals," which is short for "fractional dimensional." A fractal was of infinite length. No matter how much a fractal line was magnified, more and more smaller line segments could be seen. Like a fraction that could be continually divided to become infinitely smaller, a fractal line could be divided into infinite segments.

The main computer cores on board a starship contain the likenesses of many plants and animal life. The holodeck can draw from this storehouse when needed, to create the requested environment. To generate original images, fractal algorithms are sometimes used.

*The holodeck uses many graphics techniques, including a variation of fractal technology, to generate original worlds.*

By using fractal lines to create computer graphics, coastlines, mountains, and other natural fractal-like shapes could be generated at will. These fractals were formed by breaking lines down into smaller and smaller segments. In this *recursive* process, the same mathematical operations were applied to each new set of segments. Each pair of segments was joined at an angle, and slightly lengthened so that the original line's endpoints did not change. To accomplish this, a fractal program was first given a straight line. It then choose a point on the line at which to bend the line into two line segments. The two new line segments were then processed by the fractal program, each of them being bent into two even smaller line segments. This process continued until the line was *fractalized* to the extent required by the application.

Theoretically, the fractalizing could be performed an infinite number of times. The limitations of the PC display, however, imposed more reasonable limits on the fractalizing routine.

# Morphing

*Morphing* was a process used to animate graphics on a computer. Morphing generated the images required to cause one shape to mold itself, step by step, into another. To animate a sequence, a morphing program was given the starting and ending images—which converted them to a complex series of lines. A mathematical formula was then applied to create the steps of the transformation. As the controlling value in the formula varied from 0 to 1, each succeeding image became more like the target image.

The meticulous techniques of traditional animation (perfected by 1940) had required over 30 hand-drawn images to animate a figure smoothly for one second on the screen. Using morphing programs to computerize animation relieved these artists from performing much repetitive detail work.

Morphing techniques were put to good use in the creation of *special effects* in "motion pictures" (a popular entertainment medium in which a series of images printed on film were viewed in rapid succession, creating the illusion of motion). First a desired image (for example, a human being transforming into a different creature) would be morphed with a computer, then transferred onto motion picture film. Audiences of the day were readily entertained by such fantasies.

*In a demonstration of morphing technique, a photo of the author is transformed into a dog.*

# *Chaos*

Prior to the end of the nineteenth century, scientists thought of the universe as a place tightly governed by the rules of physics. Then it was discovered that by concentrating on the ever-faithful rules of classical physics, scientists had limited their view of the world. As a result, they had overlooked several important elements of elemental and universal behavior. Quantum theory is based entirely upon these uncertain elements, which were first hypothesized by Max Planck in 1900.

Earth scientists of the late twentieth century worked to explain one of the phenomena derived from quantum uncertainties—the phenomenon of *universal entropy*. This element was dubbed *chaos* by these scientists. This new concept of chaos was not a simple lack of order. Instead, it was an attempt to understand *flow and turbulence* in a new way. Chaos showed that even purely mathematical systems could behave in such a complicated way that one might not be able to predict what they would do under certain conditions.

For example, consider a water wheel holding a series of buckets, each of which has a small hole in the bottom to allow water to drain. When water from a fixed spigot flows into the top bucket too slowly, the water drains before the wheel can begin to move. On the other hand, when the water flow is increased to a certain point, the top bucket increases in volume enough to allow the wheel to start turning. The wheel can then settle into a continual rotation as more buckets fill with and empty of water. It would seem reasonable to assume that an even faster flow of water would result in a faster spin. Yet, if the water flow increases, the wheel's spin can *lose* its regularity and instead enter a *chaotic state*. If the wheel is spinning too quickly, for example, buckets cannot become filled, and buckets that are already full may be pulled toward the top of the wheel before they have had a chance to empty. This could slow the wheel's spin—or even reverse it.

Without considering the theory of chaos, a classical physicist would expect the wheel to settle eventually into a regular pattern of movement, as long as the water flow remained at a constant rate. The wheel might continue to turn at a constant rate, or it might *oscillate*, first turning one way and then the other, in a predictable pattern. However, Edward Lorenz (one of the early researchers in chaos theory), discovered that the wheel's pattern of movement was unpredictable—and that it would *never* settle into *any* repeating pattern.

When Lorenz graphed the variables in the equation that described the system's behavior, he made an even more interesting discovery. Although the wheel would never settle into any specific pattern, the path formed by graphing the equation *did* form a definite pattern. Organization was evident in the midst of chaos. This pattern, which looked much like a butterfly's wings became known as the *Lorenz attractor*. This "chaos," of course, is the order of the universe as presently understood. Yet twentieth-century scientists were (understandably) unwilling to sacrifice their familiar view of the world. They still had faith that conventional algebraic mathematics were the correct way to describe universal phenomena. The Lorenz attractor served, however, as evidence that another system was necessary.

Scientists discovered that many systems which could be described mathematically also had chaotic states. Some such systems included planetary weather patterns, orbits of bodies in space, and even the beating of a human heart. Prior to Lorenz's discovery, system fluctuations that did not fit with the mathematical model were ignored, considered to be nothing more than "noise" caused by some random outside influence. After Lorenz, these fluctuations were discovered to be representative of the chaotic state of the universe which could no longer be ignored.

# Nanotechnology

*I had my own experience with "nano-life" when, for a science project, I got two microbiotic nanites to interact. They bred, and accidentally invaded the computer core. Eventually Data was able to communicate with them, and the nanites agreed to help reconstruct our damaged computer files. We dropped them off on an unexplored world where they are continuing their "exploration" of the universe.*

—**Ensign Wesley Crusher,**
**Cadet, Starfleet Academy**

In 1959, Dr. Richard Feynman stated that there were no rules of physics that could prevent the creation of parts comprising only a few atoms. Because technology at that time had not progressed to a point where anything Feynman spoke of was possible, his theories were treated with indifference, and sometimes even amusement. By the end of the twentieth century, however, more and more researchers began to realize the potential of manipulating atoms to form compounds. This potential, in its way, led to the broader concept of *nanotechnology*.

For example, it was discovered that while a relatively large amount of computer data could be placed on a compact disc, that type of storage was a waste of space when compared to atomic storage. Eventually, it would become possible to create computer devices small enough to control a device the size of a bacterium.

Nanotechnology was not, however, just about creating miniaturized machines. It was also an ambitious attempt to extend the precision found at the molecular level to increasingly complex structures. In other words, nanotechnology was concerned with "building from the ground up."

Scientists soon discovered that materials made of smaller particles than those in their normal isotopes actually displayed new characteristics. For example, researcher Richard Siegal noted that palladium formed from grains five nanometers (five billionths of a meter) wide was five times harder than normal palladium. Similar studies showed that material could be made more conductive, or made to react differently to chemicals, just by varying the size of the grains with which it was constructed.

Using nanotechnology, the first *atom switch* was created. The switch was toggled by moving a single xenon atom. This type of switch revolutionized the computer industry, allowing for faster, smaller computers. It was also a step toward the reality of other types of atomic-scale electronics.

Experiments with the first atom switch began in 1987, when researchers at AT&T Bell Laboratories used a device called an STM (scanning tunneling microscope) to manipulate a few germannium atoms. An STM contained a tiny needle that conducted electricity. To manuveur atoms delicately over a conductive surface, this needle was brought so close to the surface that it almost touched it. A small electrical current was sent through the needle, causing the current to run delicately over the surface of individual atoms, mapping (and somewhat controlling) their exact position.

Researchers at IBM (International Business Machines, dominant in the twentieth-century computing industry) built on this success. They found that by applying a small pulse of electricity, individual atoms could be temporarily "bonded" to another surface. Better yet, by reapplying the electrical charge, an atom could be returned to its former position—in other words, it could be "switched" back and forth. In the nanite world of atom switching, tiny atoms appeared as "bumps" on the surface of the bonding material. When the atom was removed (the switch was turned "off"), the surface appeared almost flat.

*Almost every culture in the Federation that invented computers and computing technology independently of other worlds, did so with the ultimate intention of emulating the functions of life. Yet when I, and other scientists like myself, tried to capture the human spirit in a new kind of life, our accomplishments were met with fear and jealousy. I have never sought to design a replacement for mankind, but rather, a companion. Yet even with the best intentions, no inventor can guarantee how his or her invention will be used.*

**—Excerpted from "Often Wrong: My Life and Times" by Dr. Noonian Soong**

**Appendix**

# Galaxy-Class Starship Computing Systems

The following appendix briefly describes the computer system of a Galaxy-class starship. It is not intended as a complete text from which to study state-of-the-art computers; these will be covered thoroughly in other courses. It is merely as a reference to aid students in comparing ancient technology to our own.

# 4.0 COMPUTER SYSTEMS

## 4.1 COMPUTER SYSTEM

The main computer system of the *Enterprise* is probably the most important single operational element of the starship next to the crew. The computer is directly analogous to the autonomic nervous system of a living being, and is responsible in some way for the operation of virtually every other system of the vehicle.

Crew interface for the main computer is provided by the Library Computer Access and Retrieval System software, usually abbreviated as LCARS. LCARS provides both keyboard and verbal interface ability, incorporating highly sophisticated artificial intelligence routines and graphic display organization for maximum crew ease-of-use (See: 3.3).

### COMPUTER CORES

The heart of the main computer system is a set of three redundant main processing cores. Any of these three cores is able to handle the primary operational computing load of the entire vessel. Two of these cores are located near the center of the Primary Hull between Decks 5 and 14, while the third is located between Decks 30 and 37 in the Engineering Hull. Each main core incorporates a series of miniature subspace field generators, which creates a symmetrical (nonpropulsive) field distortion of 3350 millicochranes within the faster-than-light (FTL) core elements. This permits the transmission and processing of optical data within the core at rates significantly exceeding lightspeed.

The two main cores in the Primary Hull run in parallel clock-sync with each other, providing 100% redundancy. In the event of any failure in either core, the other core is able to instantly assume the total primary computing load for the ship with no interruption, although some secondary and recreational functions (such as holodeck simulations) may be suspended. The third core, located in the Engineering Hull, serves as a backup to the first two, and also serves the Battle Section during separated flight operations.

Core elements are based on FTL nanoprocessor units arranged into optical transtator clusters of 1,024 segments. In turn, clusters are grouped into processing modules composed of 256 clusters controlled by a bank of sixteen isolinear chips. Each core comprises seven primary and three upper levels, each level containing an average of four modules.

### CORE MEMORY

Memory storage for main core usage is provided by 2,048 dedicated modules of 144 isolinear optical storage chips. Under LCARS software control, these modules provide average dynamic access to memory at 4,600 kiloquads/sec. Total storage capacity of each module is about 630,000 kiloquads, depending on software configuration.

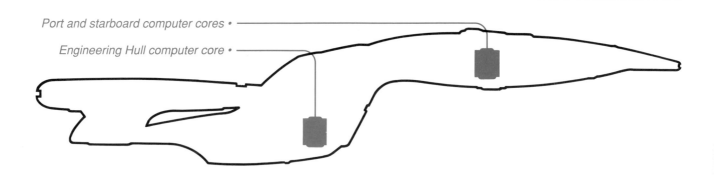

Port and starboard computer cores •

Engineering Hull computer core •

*4.1.1  Location of main computer cores*

The main cores are tied into the ship's optical data network by means of a series of MJL junction links which bridge the subspace boundary layer. There is a 12% Doppler loss in transmission rate across the boundary, but the resulting increase in processing speed from the FTL core elements more than compensates.

## SUBPROCESSORS

A network of 380 quadritronic optical subprocessors is distributed throughout both ship's sections, augmenting the main cores. Within the habitable volume of the ship, most of these subprocessors are located near main corridor junctions for easy access. While these subprocessors do not employ FTL elements, the distributed processing network improves overall system response and provides redundancy in emergency situations. Each subprocessor is linked into the optical data network, and most also have a dedicated optical link to one or more of the main cores.

The Main Bridge and the Battle Bridge each have seven dedicated and twelve shared subprocessors, which permit operations even in the event of main core failure. These bridge subprocessors are linked to the main cores by means of protected optical conduits, which provide alternate control linkages in the event of a primary optical data network failure. Further redundancy is provided by dedicated short-range radio frequency (RF) links, providing emergency data communications with the bridge. Additional dedicated subproces-

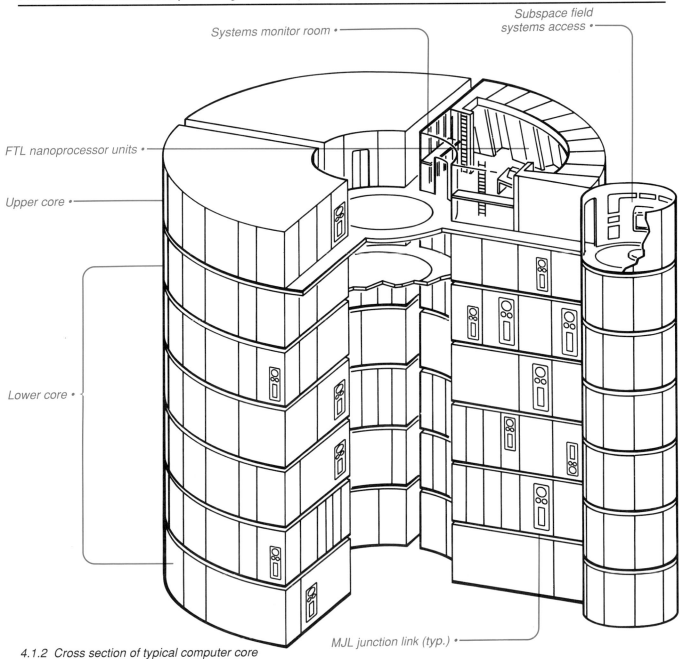

*Systems monitor room •*

*Subspace field systems access •*

*FTL nanoprocessor units •*

*Upper core •*

*Lower core •*

*MJL junction link (typ.) •*

*4.1.2 Cross section of typical computer core*

*4.1.3  Optical data network interconnects between computer cores, main bridge, and other key systems*

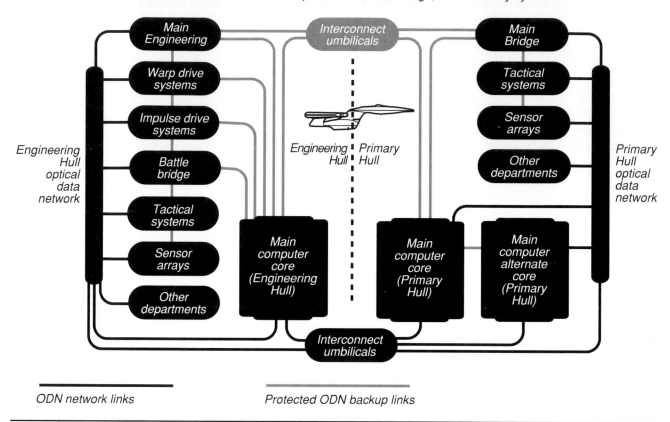

ODN network links

Protected ODN backup links

sors can be installed as needed to support mission-specific operations.

Virtually every control panel and terminal within the ship is linked to a subprocessor or directly into the optical data network. Each active panel is continually polled by LCARS at 30 millisecond intervals so that the local subprocessor and/or the main core is informed of all keyboard or verbal inputs. Each polling inquiry is followed by a 42 nanosecond compressed data stream, which provides panel update information. This data stream includes any requested visual or audio information for panel output.

Short-range RF data links are available throughout the ship to provide information transmission to portable and handheld devices such as tricorders and personal access display devices (PADD).

This integrated network of computers, subprocessors, and panels forms the "nervous system" of the ship and permits continuous realtime analysis of the ship's operating status.

The network is specifically designed to permit independent operation of remaining system elements in the event of a wide variety of partial system failures.

*We realize quite well that the* Enterprise *computer system is definitely overpowered in terms of twentieth-century computing applications. On the other hand, the history of computer technology has shown that each time a faster, more powerful computer becomes available, useful applications quickly follow to take advantage of the new machines, which in turn spurs computer designers to build still more powerful machines. One might expect that such trends will yield enormously powerful computers, which one might reasonably hope may significantly enhance the quality of life, as they apparently do for the men and women of the* Enterprise.

# 4.2 PERSONAL ACCESS DISPLAY DEVICE (PADD)

In its primary role aboard a starship, the personal access display device (PADD) is a handheld control and display terminal. Small, easily managed terminals and computers are in daily use throughout Starfleet, as a natural response to crew members' needs to (1) execute hardware functions in a variety of locations, and (2) manipulate visual information and communicate that information to others aboard ship. Access to the *Enterprise* computers and other pieces of equipment can be accomplished through the usual control displays and larger terminal screens, of course, but the PADD has become a convenient adjunct to those panels.

The standard small PADD is 10 x 15 x 1 cm and is constructed from three basic layers of imbedded circuit-composite material. All primary electronics, including multi-layer display screen, are bonded to the casing, a boronite whisker epoxy. If dropped accidentally, even from a height of 35 m, a PADD will remain undamaged. Replaceable components are limited to three, the sarium power loop, isolinear memory chip, and subspace transceiver assembly (STA).

In normal daily use, the power supply remains installed and is induction recharged. A full charge will last sixteen hours; if a PADD is about to exhaust its battery, it can set a memory flag in the main computer to transfer tasks to a working unit, or suspend them until a later time. The total memory capacity of the isolinear chips is 4.3 kiloquads. Like the tricorder, the PADD can transfer its total memory to the main computers in less than one second if the need arises. The STA is used to maintain data channels between the PADD and the *Enterprise* computers. If taken on an away mission, the PADD can also perform uplink/downlink operations and function as a transporter lock-on node. Data transmissions and computing functions can be shared with any other Starfleet device supporting the STA com protocols. As with the personal communicator, transmissions are encrypted for security purposes.

The display screen, 4.25 times larger than that of a tricorder, allows for the manipulation of control graphics, numerical data, and images by touch. Electrosensitive areas of the casing (colored brown on the standard engineering PADD) are designed for specific data movement and storage functions. They can also be used to personalize the default setup and single–crew member security restriction. An audio pickup sensor permits voice input.

The PADD's control functions mimic those of any multi-layer panel, insofar as the security restrictions for individual crew members are concerned. Properly configured with the Conn position bridge controls, a crew member can theoretically fly the *Enterprise* from a PADD while walking down a corridor. While this would be an impractical exercise due to

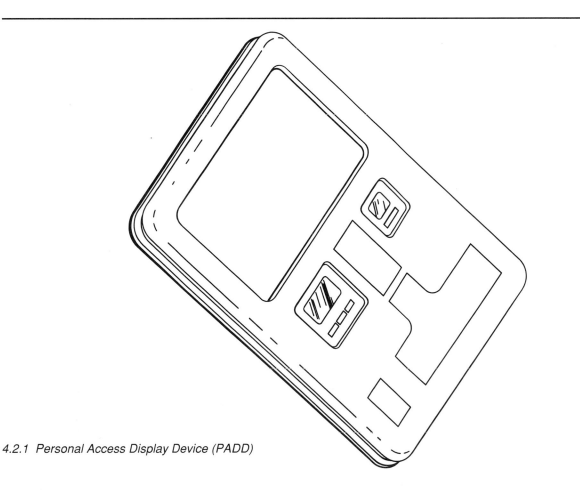

*4.2.1 Personal Access Display Device (PADD)*

PADD memory limitations and the relatively small diplay screen, it is an example of the overall multiple-option philosophy established in the *Galaxy* class starship design objectives by Starfleet's Advanced Starship Design Bureau.

This philosophy treats the starship as an integrated organism in which each component can be regarded as a cell in a body directed by a central brain, but with processing capabilities distributed throughout the neural network. Because of this, PADDs and many other handheld data devices are capable of accessing any data file or command program to which the user has authorized access.

Custom PADD configurations can be fabricated aboard the *Enterprise* or in any starship hardware replication facility equipped with custom isolinear circuit programming capabilities.

---

*Guy Vardaman, who among other things occasionally plays a crew member seen in the background of scenes in the* Enterprise *corridors, says that he and his fellow extras sometimes refer to PADDs as "hall passes." The acronym PADD was suggested by* Star Trek *research consultant Richard Arnold during the early days of the series.*

---

# 4.3  ISOLINEAR OPTICAL CHIPS

Isolinear optical chips are the primary software and data storage medium employed throughout the *Enterprise* computer systems. These nanotech devices represent a number of significant advances over the crystal memory cards used in earlier systems.

These new chips make use of single-axis optical crystal layering to achieve subwavelength switching distances. Nanopulse matrix techniques yield a total memory capacity of 2.15 kiloquads per chip in standard holographic format.

Like earlier crystal memory devices, isolinear chips optimize memory access by employing onboard nanoprocessors. In these new devices, however, higher processing speeds permit individual chips to manage data configuration independent of LCARS control, thus reducing system access time by up to 7%. Additionally, the chip substrate is infused with trace quantities of superconductive platinum/irridium, which permits FTL optical data transmission when energized by the core's subspace flux. This results in a dramatic 335% increase in processing speed when used in one of the main computer cores.

Isolinear chips can be ruggedized with the application of a protective tripolymer sealant over the refractive interface surface. This allows the chip to be handled without protective gloves. When so treated, isolinear chips are used as a convenient form of information transport. Many portable data-handling devices such as tricorders, PADDs, and optical chip readers are able to read and write to standard format isolinear chips.

4.3.1  *Isolinear optical chip*

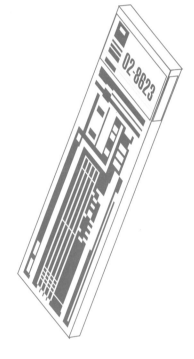

---

*Isolinear optical chips were invented by veteran* Star Trek *writer Dorothy Fontana for the episode "The Naked Now." The design of the prop is intended to reflect the original "microtape" data cartridges used in the original series, but in a much more compact and powerful form. Ironically, those original props are about the same size as the 3.5-inch Macintosh diskettes which we used when writing this book.*

## Index

# *Index*

157

*161*

# STAR TREK®
## THE NEXT GENERATION™

# TECHNICAL MANUAL

## By RICK STERNBACH and MICHAEL OKUDA
### With a special introduction by
## GENE RODDENBERRY

★

Written by Rick Sternbach and Michael Okuda, the technical advisors to STAR TREK:
THE NEXT GENERATION, the STAR TREK: THE NEXT GENERATION TECHNICAL MANUAL
takes you on a guided tour through the *U.S.S. ENTERPRISE*™ NC-1701D.

From the bridge to the shuttlebays, from the transporter room to crew's quarters, the
STAR TREK: THE NEXT GENERATION TECHNICAL MANUAL provides a never-before-seen
glimpse at the inner workings of the most incredible Starship ever conceived.

Full of diagrams, technical schematics, and ship's plans, the TECHNICAL MANUAL
takes a look at STAR TREK'S awesome technology - from phasers to the warp drive to
the incredible holodeck.

A must for all fans, this is the one book that examines the full spectrum of technology
behind the fantastic STAR TREK: THE NEXT GENERATION universe.

POCKET
BOOKS

AVAILABLE IN TRADE PAPERBACK FROM POCKET BOOKS